Battlefield
of the
mind

for Kids

JOYCE MEYER

with Karen Moore

FaithWords

NEW YORK NASHVILLE

FaithWords
Hachette Book Group
1290 Avenue of the Americas, New York, NY 10104
faithwords.com
twitter.com/faithwords

First Published in 2006
Revised Edition: March 2018

FaithWords is a division of Hachette Book Group, Inc. The FaithWords name and logo are trademarks of Hachette Book Group, Inc.

The publisher is not responsible for websites (or their content) that are not owned by the publisher.

The Hachette Speakers Bureau provides a wide range of authors for speaking events. To find out more, go to www.hachettespeakersbureau.com or call (866) 376-6591.

Library of Congress Cataloging-in-Publication Data has been applied for.

ISBNs: 978-1-5460-3321-9 (trade paperback), 978-1-5460-3290-8 (ebook)

Printed in the United States of America

LSC-C

Printing 6, 2020

contents

Introduction

What is the battlefield of the mind and how does it impact you? Well, as you already know, your mind is filled with lots of thoughts. What's for dinner? What will I be when I grow up? What game will I play today?

Those thoughts are not bad.

But sometimes our thoughts are bad, and they can lead us down a dangerous path. Things like worry, doubt, fear, and negativity can easily creep into our minds. And then they make us act differently. They make us act less than God would want us to. They make us forget how awesome God is and how God can handle our problems.

No one really wants to lose the battle in his or her mind. We all would much rather live like winners. But, there are some things we have to do if we want to win the battle. We have to make sure our thinking is right and in line with God's Word.

In this book, I plan to help you win that battle. I

will give you the tools of God's Word to help you win. I want you to think of all of the great things God has in store for you. I want you to think of all of the amazing promises God has given to you through His Word—your Bible. I want you to think of all of the ways God has helped people—and know that God will help you, too.

Make up your mind that you will win the battle—and I will show you how!

Let's get started.

Chapter 1

Thoughts Have Power

Did you know that your thoughts have power? No, not the type of power to make you leap over buildings like a superhero, but the type of power that can make you happy, or sad, or hopeful. What you think about influences what you do and how you live. Want to be happy? Think more positive

3

and happy thoughts. Want to live like God wants you to? Think more about God and God's promises.

In Philippians 4:8, God gave us some great examples of things to think about. We're told, "Think about the things that are good and worthy of praise. Think about the things that are true and honorable and right and pure and beautiful and respected." The author goes on to say that if we do that, it is God who will give us His peace.

You see thinking about good and right and pure and beautiful things gives you the right mind set. Your mind is focused on good so you will have peace.

If you want more peace in your life, consider what you've been thinking about. Refocus your thoughts on God things and you will get more peace.

Getting Your Thoughts in Shape

In today's world, it is easy to have a million things running through your mind. You have to remember to do what your mom tells you to do. You have to think about your homework assignments. You also talk to your friends and want to remember what they say. And then, you have your own thoughts—thoughts about what you want to do later today or this week; perhaps you think a lot about what you want to do when you grow up. How can you stay focused on God things when you have so many other thoughts running through your head? How can you do what God wants you to do when you also want to please your friends and others?

In my book *Battlefield of the Mind*, which I wrote for adults, I help them create tools that will be useful in getting their minds straight. Let's make a mental tool kit and put some of these ideas into it.

- **Read your Bible:** Well, that seems simple enough, but where do you start? Let's look at Romans 12:2: It says, "Do not change yourselves to be like the people of this world, but be changed within by a new way of thinking. Then you will be able to decide what God wants for you; you will know what is good and pleasing to him and what is perfect."

Okay, you read that, now let's look at it again. It says to *not* follow the crowd, not just make a choice because everyone else has. You can be yourself, and sometimes that means making different decisions from your friends' decisions!

So, What Should You Do?

Let's think a moment about why you want to be like your friends. Usually, you want to be like other people because you admire them, or think they are cool, or think they're very special in some way. Those are fine reasons to want to be like someone else.

Go Look at your Bible!

But what if the person you admire decides to do something you don't agree with? What if your friends want to be mean to the new kid at school? You know you should be nice and welcome the kid. But you also don't want your friends to be mad at you. What would you do? Would you stick up for the new kid? Or would you go along with your friends and make fun of the new student? Or would you just be quiet and say nothing?

When you take the Bible's advice and look within yourself to discover

BRaVO FOR You!

what's true for you, it may mean disagreeing with your friends and even choosing to not be friends for a while.

This would be you thinking in a new way, looking at what is right for you. Thinking that way helps you know clearly what God wants for you and helps you choose a way that will be good and pleasing to Him.

- **Give yourself permission to think your own thoughts**. You don't have to be like everyone else—and you don't have to think like everyone else, either.

- **The Bible gives us patience and encouragement so that we can have hope**. When you hope to make good decisions and have good thoughts, this tool will help you every time.

■ **Give yourself an opportunity to think again—or to review your thoughts.** The good news about growing up and changing your thinking is that you can always think again. You have another chance to make a better choice than you did the last time. You're never stuck with having to think only one way. With Jesus, you've always got another chance.

■ **Think about Jesus' example.** (See Hebrews 12:3.) When you're making a choice, do your best to imagine what you think Jesus might do or how He might act in the situation you're facing. Go back to your friend who wanted to be mean to the new kid. Think about it through Jesus' eyes. What would He tell your friend? What would He tell you? Think about those things.

■ **Don't be tricked.** In Hebrews, there's a reminder to hold on to the things you were taught. Don't let strange teachings take you down the wrong road. You have information at your fingertips these days. Just because you hear some "information" on TV or read it on social media doesn't mean it is true. You don't have to follow everything you hear. Your heart should be strengthened by

God's grace (see Hebrews 13:9). In other words, you have the answer within you. God has already given you what you need.

Now you've got a pretty full toolbox. If you carry it with you wherever you go, it will help you think correctly. It will help you out on the different battlefields you come across: in the schoolyard, in the classroom, and at the party at your friend's house. You need your mind to be as healthy as possible, and being equipped is only part of the answer.

Let's move on and see what's showing up on your mind.

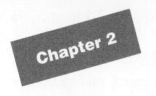

Chapter 2

What's On Your Mind?

I can't study for a science test. I'm going to the movies tonight!

SCIENCE TEST TOMORROW!

Have you ever had a tough time making a good decision? You have several choices and you want to pick more than one. For instance, you may want to go to a movie with your friends. But you also have a science test tomorrow. You could stay home and study. Even though studying for the test seems like the right choice, you still want to hang out

with your friends. Your mind is confused. You are in the middle of a battle trying to make a choice.

The battle for your mind and your thinking will go on your whole life, but it's going to feel especially crazy now while you're in school. Your mind will likely jump and hop and swerve in a hundred directions, leaving you unsure about what you really think and feel and what your options are.

I call this having a "confused mind," and you probably know what I mean. When your mind is confused,
it wanders all over the place looking for answers. Your
mind just doesn't know what is normal and how to focus
on the right direction. It's in a no-win situation, because
it doesn't know, so it can't win. The Bible puts it this way
in James 1:5–8: "If any of you needs wisdom, you should
ask God for it. He is generous and enjoys giving to all
people, so he will give you wisdom. But when you

SOMETIMES I THINK FIVE OR SIX THINGS ... OH ME! ask God, you must believe and not doubt. Anyone who doubts is like a wave in the sea, blown up and down by the wind. Such doubters are thinking two different things at the same time, and they cannot decide about anything they do."

Does that sound like you in any way? Do you ever think two different things at the same time and aren't sure what to do?

So, what do you do? According to James, you should ask God for wisdom. What is wisdom? It's help in great big capital letters ..H E L P!! You tell God that you don't know what you should do in the situation you're in, and you ask Him to help you make a good choice.

Making Confusing Choices

Let's say you're confused about whether to go to a party or not. You know that the popular girl who is having the party is kind of boy-crazy. You know that she has an older brother who may crash the party with some of his friends, and if your mother knew that, she wouldn't agree to let you go at all. You think that maybe if your mom doesn't know about the older brother, it could be okay and you could still go to the party.

Your mind starts to spin its web of confusion. Before you know it, you're trapped like the victim of a spider as you try to decide what to do.

Let's pretend you're now reading someone else's story and you can choose your own ending to this situation. We'll set the story up and then you can choose ending number one, number two, or number three.

The Story

"Mom, I've been invited to a party at my friend Shari's house. It's her birthday, and she's just having a few kids over for pizza and games. Will you be able to take me over on Friday night and pick me up? Is it okay if I go?"

"Will Shari's parents be home?" Mom asks.

"Oh, sure, Mom. They're really nice people, and I'm sure you'd like them. Shari said you could call her mom about the party if you want to."

"Well, I guess that won't be necessary," Mom says with a smile. "You just go ahead and have a good time. I'll take you somewhere tomorrow to pick up a little birthday gift for her."

"Thanks, Mom. That would be great."

As Sally leaves the kitchen after talking with her mom, she remembers her concern about Shari's older brother showing up with older kids. She debates whether to tell her mom that part.

Sally goes up to her room and texts her friend Shari. She tells her that she'll be allowed to come to the birthday party, and her friend is pleased. Sally asks if Shari's parents will be there, and her friend says, "Well, no, they'll be out for part of the evening, but my older brother will be here, and he's eighteen, so it will be okay."

Sally now has to decide...

Ending One:

Sally deletes the messages and decides she'll just keep that information to herself. After all, what could go wrong? Her mom will never have to know. Shari's mom must think her son is responsible at eighteen.

But Sally has an awful time at the party. She is very uncomfortable, wondering if something bad will happen. Sally looks at every older kid suspiciously. She wonders if someone will get into a fight or start drinking, and there won't be an adult to protect them. She decides to just call her mom and ask her to pick her up early. No use in staying at the party if she can't have fun.

Ending Two:

Sally decides that she'd better tell her mom that Shari's parents will not be at the party. She knows her mom would not be comfortable with her going under those circumstances, and she wouldn't feel right not letting her know.

"Mom," Sally says quietly, "I just found out that Shari's parents will be out for part of the evening while the birthday party is going on. She says her older brother, who is eighteen, will be there, though, to watch over things. Is it still okay for me to go?"

"Sally, I know how much you'd like to go to this

party, but I don't feel good about a group of kids being in the house unsupervised. I don't think Shari's brother would be much help if someone became ill or got into any trouble. Would you mind if I call Shari's mother to discuss this before we decide?"

"Oh, that would be great. I'm sure Mrs. Peterson would be happy to talk with you about it."

Sally's mother calls Mrs. Peterson and finds out that they will actually only be missing about the first hour of the party. Along with her son, she's called her mother, Shari's grandmother, to also be there until she gets home.

Sally is allowed to go to the party with a clear conscience, and she has a good time.

Ending Three:

Sally hangs up the phone and decides she'd better tell her mom that Shari's parents won't be home after all. When she does tell her mom, her mom says that there is no way Sally can go, because she's just too young to go to an unsupervised party, and Shari's older brother doesn't qualify as a good parenting model.

Sally gets angry with her mother and decides to sneak out and go to the party anyway. She tells her mom she's staying overnight with another friend who was not allowed to go to the party. Her mom thinks that's a nice alternative choice and takes Sally to her friend Margie's house.

Margie and Sally go to the party, even though neither of them is really allowed to go Sally feels a twinge of guilt.

They go to the party, and things seem fine at first until one kid gets mad at another one and starts a food fight. Before Sally knows what is happening, food is flying through the air, and pizza is sticking to the ceiling faster than Shari's brother can get things under control.

Sally feels really bad about the house, and just as she's trying to convince Margie that they should get out of there, Shari's parents come home. They stop the party and call all the kids into the living room. They tell them that they will be calling all of their parents to set up times for each kid to come back and help clean up the mess. Sally's heart sinks.

Sally's Confused Mind

Why did Sally have a confused mind? Did she know the right thing to do?

Sally knew in her heart what she should have done. She became confused when she tried to give herself reasons or excuses for thinking something other than what she knew was the truth. God did not give us a spirit of confusion (see 1 Corinthians 14:33), so we can know right away that confusion means the devil is tempting us to do the wrong thing.

If you know what to do in your heart, that's God's Spirit trying to help you make a good choice. If you don't want to hear what God has to say, you can find some pretty easy excuses floating around in your brain, and they'll always give you permission to do the wrong thing. When those bad thoughts pop into your head, you need to ask God for help right away. Get rid of those thoughts quickly. They only lead to helping you make more and more excuses about why you should do something. Even though God may let you know it's not the right thing to do, if you keep pondering, you just might end up doing it. Get rid of confusion and doubt quickly. Don't let your mind go down that road. Think about what God would want you to do.

Dealing with Doubt

Another way you can get a confused mind is when you walk in doubt instead of in truth or in joy or in love.

Doubt crops up like ants at a picnic anytime you leave food sitting on the blanket. Your job is to see it as quickly as possible and cover up or get rid of that food. Doubt can send your mind down a long, dreary path. It will have you thinking lots of hopeless and negative thoughts. It's like once a seed is planted in your mind, doubt will make it grow into a big tree. That's why it is so important to catch the seed before it grows. It's important to take the seed of doubt out of your mind while it is still little. It's much easier to throw away a seed than to throw away a tree.

God gave you a tool to help you get rid of doubt. It's called faith. And faith simply means that you believe and trust in something or someone. When you feel happy and confident and everything is going your way, you don't doubt much. You are usually thankful and grateful. You can believe and trust that God is taking care of you.

But when you are having a bad day, you just failed the math test, and you didn't play well in gym, doubt comes in and camps in your mind.

Doubt will play all kinds of tricks on you. It will tell

you that you deserved to fail that math test because you didn't study hard enough, and not only that, it will convince you that you will never be good at math, so why even try?

Doubt Is the Villain

Doubt wants to control your thoughts so that you stop making an effort to do the right thing and settle for less than what God has for you. If doubt can hold you back right now while you're in the fifth grade, imagine the fun it can have when you get to high school!

What Can You Do?

So what are you going to do? What tool do you have to get rid of doubt? Like we talked about on the last page, it's faith—the amount of faith God has given you. The more you put that faith into action and believe God, the bigger your faith will grow. The more you learn about God and know God's Word, the bigger your faith will grow. When you really believe God's Word, you'll have the faith to do what God says. And big faith can push away doubt faster and quicker than small faith. That's one of the main reasons it is important to grow your faith, increase in wisdom, and praise God so that you'll be stronger and better equipped to fight off doubt when it comes in.

First Peter 5:8–10 (New Century Version) says this: "Control yourselves and be careful! The devil, your enemy, goes around like a roaring lion looking for someone to eat. Refuse to give in to him by standing strong in your faith…God who gives all grace will make everything right. He

POP!

will make you strong and support you and keep you from falling."

So how big is your faith today? Learn to lean and depend on God to help you resist doubt.

A Sleepy Mind

When you feel sleepy, you're not really interested in what is going on around you. You may not be able to pay attention in English class, you may not be able to pay attention in church, or you may not care too much about what your best friend is saying right that second. Being sleepy means you're not alert.

I call this condition a "passive mind." That means you're not really thinking about any one thing and you're not alert. Sometimes you are sleepy, and I'm not talking about being tired from a long day. I'm talking about not keeping on the alert for the enemy and not being on the alert for what God wants you to know. You have to watch out for the things that will fill up those empty spaces in your head. When your head is empty, it's easy to fill it up with all kinds of unhealthy thoughts.

What Can You Do to Wake Up?

For starters, you can be sure that your mind is full of good thoughts. When good thoughts are cramming

your brain, there's no room for nasty thoughts to hang out. They try to get in, and they see the God thoughts you have, and they just don't bother sticking around. Your best tool to fill yourself with good thoughts is to study the Bible and pray. This will help you keep God thoughts in your mind.

You might think it's okay to NOT pray and read the Bible and stay sleepy (or passive) as long as you're not getting into any trouble or doing anything that might be considered wrong. But are you?

Sometimes problems march right into your head and stick around simply because they can see that nothing else is going on. It's easy for your problems to play games in your mind, because you've given them a whole lot of space to do so. Nothing else was happening in your mind. Just as when the door going out to the backyard is left open and bugs start to fly in, you left your mind open for bad thoughts and problems and other negative ideas to come inside.

Why Does Reading the Bible Help?

Ephesians 6: 10–13 says this: "Finally, be strong in the Lord and in His great power. Put on the full armor of God so that you can fight against the devil's evil tricks.

Our fight is not against people on earth but against
the rulers and authorities and powers of this world's
darkness, against the spiritual pow-
ers of evil in the heavenly
world. That is why you
need to put on God's full
armor. Then on the day of
evil you will be able
to stand strong."

Reading the Bible
is part of putting on
your armor, or your
protective suit, so
that you know how to
fight off the evil thoughts
that come your way.
When you're sleepy,
you're not a very good

fighter. You're not very strong or alert. God's Word will give you tools to fight with.

What Is Prayer, and How Can It Help the Way You Think?

You've probably been saying certain kinds of prayers since you were little. You've said prayers at night, perhaps with your parents, and you've said prayers at dinner. Now and then, you may have uttered a prayer of thanks when you did better on a test than you thought you would. By now you know that there are lots of ways to pray and different kinds of prayers.

As you keep growing, it's understandable that a lot of your prayers will be in the form of requests, asking God's help with school or family matters or friends. Those are great prayers.

Some of your prayers may be gratitude prayers, where you thank God for the good things in your life. The kind of prayer we want to talk about right now, though, is the kind that helps shape how you think.

Asking for God's Will

You come to God in this kind of prayer specifically to see if you can line up your thinking with His plans for

your life. You're really putting
yourself aside and asking for
God's plans to happen. That's
a very grown-up prayer, and
many adults even have trouble
with that one. If
you want to
learn to think
according to God's
plan and purpose
for your life, though, this is a
great prayer to pray.

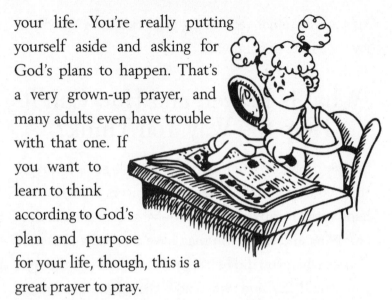

Let's find an example of this kind of prayer.

The first thing to do when syncing up with God's
plans is to take a look inside yourself. What are you
thinking about? What's in your heart? What are you
praying about?

This kind of heart-to-heart prayer is one of the most
special prayers you can pray. This one tells God that
you're serious about getting the very best answer possible and that you really want to think more like Jesus.
This one says you want your thoughts to be right, and
you want to think as clearly as possible.

Here's an example of the kind of prayer we're
talking about. See what Joe decides to do.

Joe just found out at dinner that his dad's company

is moving to another city. He and his family will have to move to a new town in one month. Joe is not happy. In fact, he's mad. His friends are here, and he is super involved with stuff at school. He does *not* want to go.

He told his dad and mom that he didn't think this move was a good idea. After yelling at the dinner table that he wasn't going to go, he found himself in his room sulking. After a while, his mom came upstairs and knocked on his door.

She told him she was sorry that they would have to move, but there really wasn't much they could do since his dad's work was the main support for the family. Joe kept sulking, but as his mom was preparing to leave the room, she offered him one more suggestion. "Why don't you talk to God about it?" she said.

At first, Joe wasn't so sure he really cared about what God thought, but as the evening went on, he decided he didn't really have much to lose. After all, come tomorrow, he'd have to tell all of his friends that he'd be moving nearly eight hours away. His first tries at prayer didn't go very well.

His anger kept getting in the way. He wanted God to change this whole thing so they could stay put. Still not feeling any better with his prayers, he decided to stop being angry and just tell God what was in his heart.

At that point, Joe's prayers changed. His new prayer sounded like this:

> *Hi, God,*
> *I'm not feeling very happy right now. My dad says we have to move to another city, and I know I'm going to miss my friends. If there's any way You can change things so we don't have to move, I'd sure like that. But either way, if you could help me get through this and even help the way I think about it, that would be good. I know You want the best for my whole family. Thanks for listening.*
> *Amen.*

Do you see what Joe did right? You can do this, too! This prayer shows Joe's effort to get his thinking lined up with God's thinking. It may take some time for him to do that, but he's made a start, and God will help him. And He'll do the same thing for you.

Be sure to include prayers for "right thinking" in your toolbox.

Chapter 3

Gossip! Gossip! Gossip!

Have you ever played a game called Telephone, where one person whispers something into the ear of the person seated by them, and then they pass the same words along to the person next to them, and the original idea goes all around the room until the last person is supposed to say what the sentence was?

For example, I might start the game with something like, "Chocolate sauce is really great with ice cream, bananas, and mixed nuts." By the time it goes around the ten people in the chain, the person who tells us the sentence says something like, "The truck driver put on his brakes when he saw some ice so he wouldn't get creamed like a banana in a rut."

Sometimes you carry around things in your mind that you think someone said or you heard from someone else, and then you worry about it, and later on you find out it wasn't even true. You might even find out that by the time the gossip gets to you, it has completed changed from what was said in the beginning.

This Thing Called Gossip

Let's look at something that goes on all the time at school…this thing called gossip. What if someone spreads gossip about you? How should you think about that? Then, too, what if someone tries to share gossip with you? What should you do about that?

Gossip is usually mean-spirited. Someone who starts gossip isn't usually being kind about someone else. Gossip is generally meant to bring somebody down or make them upset. Usually it happens when one kid is angry at another or jealous over something.

Whatever the reason, it's a very nasty thing indeed, and it hurts many people.

The Bible says in Proverbs 18:8: "The words of a gossip are like tasty bits of food. People like to gobble them up."

In another proverb, it says, "The person who tells one side of a story seems right, until someone else comes and asks questions" (Proverbs 18:17).

Choices about Gossip

It's important for you to watch out for gossip, whatever form it takes. What choices do you have if someone gossips to you or about you?

1. TELL THEM YOUR MIND IS BUSY THINKING ABOUT MORE IMPORTANT THINGS.

2. URGE THEM ON TO TELL YOU MORE.

3. DEFEND THE PERSON THEY ARE TALKING ABOUT.

You can tell the gossiper to stop. Tell that person that you really don't want to hear anything bad. You can even change the conversation to something good.

If you're tempted to listen, think about the golden rule: Do unto others as you would have them do unto you (see Matthew 7:12). You also need to remember that those who will talk about others to you will also talk about you to others.

Practice a Mind-set Like Jesus

So, when someone comes near you with some tasty morsels of gossip, it's time to practice having a mind-set that is more like Jesus' mind-set. Before you know it, you'll discover that people will come to realize that you don't like to hear their gossip, and they'll stop trying to share it. The gossip then might be, "Don't bother telling Jack. He doesn't like to hear gossip. He's a Christian who really is trying to act like Jesus." That's okay, though. You don't mind being thought of as someone who acts like Jesus, do you?

What If the Gossip Is about You?

Now, what if the hot gossip is about you? Proverbs 26:20 says, "Without wood, a fire will go out, and without gossip, quarreling will stop." In other words, if you don't fan the flames or react in a way that makes people think what they've heard is right, it will soon go away. When whoever started gossip about you realizes that they really didn't get the result they hoped for, they'll likely stop doing it. It simply won't be worth the effort for them to keep going. The fire will die out.

So why is gossip so destructive? After all, what's the big deal about passing along something you heard about someone, even if you don't know whether or not it's true? Let's play a little game of truth or lies. Your job is to decide whether each of the following statements is true or false. Then you have to decide whether you buy into the statement or not. Ready?

Statement One:

If I want to be class president, I'll do whatever it takes to win. I don't care about the other guy. My job is to be a winner.

Statement Two:

If I want to be popular, I have to do what the popular kids are doing, even if I don't really agree with them.

Statement Three:

If I share bad news about someone else, it makes me look better because I seem to be part of the in crowd.

Being a Winner

So, all of you hoping to be class president, or part of the swim team, or anything else where you have to compete to get in, what do you say? Is it more important to win and not worry about the other guy? Do you just do whatever it takes, even if it isn't totally right?

THE BEST WAY TO WIN

What would popular gossip say to do? What would Jesus say to do? How should you think about it?

What Is Right Thinking?

You have to start with right thinking. You have to start with Jesus and a mind-set that can give you clear direction. Galatians 5:25–26 puts it this way: "We get our new life from the Spirit, so we should follow the Spirit. We must not be proud or make trouble with each other or be jealous of each other."

When you compete, do it fairly. Do everything based on your values and principles and what you believe God is telling you to do. Do it in a way that will make you feel God's blessing because you are acting according to His will and purpose for your life. You are doing what God wants you to do.

Be a Winner in God's Eyes

Do what it takes to be a winner in God's eyes, and you will come out on top every time. The good news is that you don't have to be a star to win with Him. You're already His light in the world. You're His success story every time you choose to be on His team and do what makes God smile. At the end of the day, you should be more committed to winning with God than winning without Him.

Being Popular

It's great to be popular. It's nice to be someone whom everyone knows and wants to be with and invites over. It's great, or so it seems to everyone on the outside, but what's really happening on the inside? What's going on in the minds of those who want to look like they'd do anything to stay popular?

Sometimes being popular means that you think you have power. You can get what you want, get other people to do what you want, feel important at school, and so on. When you're the popular person, you sometimes forget to be the person who also can think and act independently of the group. There's a risk to being popular. You don't ever want to forget who you are and that you can think for yourself.

The Trouble with Groupthink

Today, a lot of gangs exist in this country. They exist in part because kids have bought into the idea that certain members of the group have power, and that if they want to have any power, too, they have to be part of the gang.

They believe that if the group does it, it must be all right. This same message goes for little groups at school, or even church. Be very careful of little groups that try to make everyone think alike and act the same way.

It's All Wrong Thinking

Galatians 6:1–5 reads: "If someone in your group does something wrong, you who are spiritual should go to that person and gently help make him right again. But be careful because you might be tempted to sin, too. By helping each other with your troubles, you truly obey the law of Christ. If anyone thinks he is important when he really is not, he is only fooling himself. Each person should judge his own actions and not compare himself with others. Then he can be proud for what he himself has done. Each person must be responsible for himself."

It's okay to be popular. It's okay to be well liked. But be liked for who you really are as a child of God. Be a leader in sharing your smile, your kindness, your friendship, and your beliefs with those around you. Telling the truth of who you are will give you the freedom to be yourself. When you don't agree with popular opinions, it's okay to say so. In fact, you must say so in order to be true to yourself.

How Do You Think?

How do you think? What helps you know when it's better to be outside of the in crowd and not try so hard to get in? When you think about it, you've got the most powerful information the world has ever known. You've got the key to salvation and eternal life.

Your Greatest Weapon for the Battle

One of your greatest weapons is the Word. John 8:31 says: "So Jesus said to the Jews who believed in him, 'If you continue to obey my teaching, you are truly my followers. Then you will know the truth. And the truth will make you free.'"

You must get the knowledge of God's truth in you and renew your mind with His Word. If you want to be smart, to have knowledge, to know things, do so from the Word of God. Know Him, and you will have real power.

Get to Know Jesus

If you're not sure about this, get to know Jesus. If you don't know Jesus very well, ask your family or a pastor to tell you more about Him. He's your friend. He's ready to guide you anytime you ask for His help. He died for you. He loves you just as you are. Don't be fooled. Don't let anyone try to change your mind. Use the real wisdom that comes from prayer and reading your Bible, and keep your heart and mind on Christ Jesus.

If you want to share any news, share the Good News of knowing Jesus by living and acting like Him. You've got a calling to do that. Leave gossip and bad news and wrong thinking to someone else. You don't need it. Shine your light wherever you go—at school, at home, in your community and church.

Chapter 4

Whoa! Watch Out for Things That Can Poison You!

If you've watched any Star Wars movies or even any TV at all, you're aware of the battle that goes on all around us between good and evil. We're bombarded with things that can take our minds off track, and we don't need an encounter with Darth Vader to make it happen. Everything from the Internet, to music, to TV commercials attacks your thinking and makes it harder for you to figure out what's really good and what isn't.

So, How Do You Protect Your Mind?

It's important to protect your mind from the things that can poison you, the same way you protect your body from germs. You wash your hands before meals so that you don't get germs in your food that can harm your body. You've been taught safety rules and health rules and other rules to protect you when you go out into the world. Well, guess what? Your mind needs extra protection, too. Your mind needs protection from the garbage and bad thoughts that can enter it. These poisonous thoughts can act like a germ and poison your mind if you let them stay too long. You need to wear the helmet of salvation everywhere you go (remember the full armor of God in Ephesians 6:10–13?).

You need to put on the whole armor of God.
Ephesians 6: 11-17 says this:

Put on the full armor of God so that you can fight against the devil's evil tricks. Our fight is not against people on earth but against the rulers and authorities and the powers of this world's darkness, against the spiritual powers of evil in the heavenly world. That is why you need to put on God's full armor...So stand strong; with the belt of truth tied around your waist and the protection of right living on your chest. On your feet wear the Good News of peace to help you stand strong. And also use the shield of faith with which you can stop all the burning arrows of the Evil One. Accept God's salvation as your helmet, and take the sword of the Spirit, which is the word of God.

Getting You All Bent Out of Shape

What are some of the things that can try to poison your mind? Let's look at a few examples and see what can be done to get them out of your head.

- Who do you think you are? You can't share your faith with anyone. They'll think you're crazy and super spiritual.
- Why are you praying about passing a test? Praying won't do you any good.
- You know you don't really have to get up to go to church. Your friends get to sleep in on Sunday morning.
- You don't really think your parents believe all this religious stuff, do you?

Poisonous Thoughts

Poisonous thoughts are the thoughts the enemy uses to try to confuse you into thinking that all the beliefs you have aren't real, that God isn't real and you're silly to believe in Him. If you allow them to take over your thinking, you won't know what you believe anymore.

As a Christian, you have to decide what you are going to believe. Even though you're young, your faith is still strong. Like seeds of truth planted inside you, they'll keep growing your whole life if you nurture them.

So What Should You Do?

Get ready to pray and pray boldly. If you believe in the power of prayer, you can ask God to deal with those poisonous thoughts that crop up in your mind. Each time one pops into your head, ask God to help you. Trust and believe that God hears you and watch your thoughts change from bad and negative to good and positive. Keep praying until there are different thoughts in your head—God thoughts.

Who Are You?

■ **The truth is that you know exactly who you are.** You're a child of God, and you can share your faith because God will strengthen you to do it. When the time is right for the person you share with, they'll grow in faith, too. That's the way it works. We're in a family that keeps reaching out to bring others into the family, too. You want others to know God like you know God so they can have joy and God's promises, too.

■ **Praying is the best weapon you have.** You should pray about any situation. You can pray about a test, about a friend, about your family, and anything else that you feel is important to pray about. It's one of the side benefits of being connected to a loving Father. Pray anytime. Pray all of the time.

- **You belong in a church, a community of believers.** Church is where you find people like you and where you can learn and grow together. You may not always feel like getting up to go to church on a given Sunday morning or even during the week. However, you've probably already discovered that when you do go, you feel so much better the rest of the day or week. Your heart is lighter, you have more peace, and the world looks a little bit better. Let your friends sleep in. You need to get to church!

- **If your parents are Christians, they can help you.** You've probably been going to church with your parents since you were born. You have been placed in their care so that they could help nurture your faith, as well as your mind and your body. Your parents are your allies, and they are praying for you to grow and become even more of who God means for you to be. If this is true for you, then bless your parents and thank them for what they've given you. They can help you continue to grow. Feel free to ask them how they grew to know and love God. If your parents are not Christians, you can be a light for them. Keep praying for them, and keep learning all you can about God. One day, you may be able to share more about God with your parents. They will be grateful for your example.

In the future, when those poisonous thoughts start to nag you, lie to you, and make you feel confused inside, remember this: You can send them packing with your bold faith. Pray and remember all you've learned about God. If need be, repeat some of your favorite Scriptures. This will get your mind back on track and send those poisonous thoughts away

The Bible says this:

Let everyone see that you are gentle and kind. The Lord is coming soon. Do not worry about anything, but pray and ask God for everything you need, always giving thanks. And God's peace, which is so great we cannot understand it, will keep your hearts and minds in Christ Jesus. (Philippians 4:5–7)

Here's a little checklist that you can use to help you when you feel confused by poisonous thoughts. It gives you some Scripture references to read, some ideas to help clear your thinking, and some journaling space where you can jot down an idea or two of your own.

What to Do When Poisonous Thoughts Pop into Your Mind Checklist

1. Pray: "Dear Jesus, please protect my thoughts and my mind. Please stand between me and any lies that might come into my head."

2. Say out loud: "In the name of Jesus, I come against all poisonous spirits."

3. Read Philippians 4:8–9. It's full of nice things to think about. It says: "Brothers and sisters, think about the things that are good and worthy of praise. Think about the things that are true and honorable and right and pure and beautiful and respected. Do what you learned and received from me, what I told you, and what you saw me do. And the God who gives peace will be with you."

4. Talk with your mom or dad or a friend about any confusion you have.

5. Talk to your pastor or Sunday school teacher about your thoughts.

6. Trust that God is with you all the time and will hear your prayers concerning anything on your heart and mind.

7. "Change your thoughts and you change your world," says Norman Vincent Peale.

8. When in need, repeat any of the steps on this list.

9. Write down your thoughts and concerns so you can pray about them. Put a journal beside your bed and write down your thoughts, the date, and what you prayed or what you felt concerned about. Then check back to discover how God answered your prayers. Be sure to include the answers in your journal, as well because they will renew and strengthen you when the need arises again.

10. Remember who you are, and focus your thoughts on Jesus.

Does Access to Media Harm You?

I just can't leave this chapter without also talking about media. I mentioned it at the beginning of this chapter, but I want to know that you realize your mind is being bombarded with a lot of information, and some of it is wrapped in very pretty packaging to get you to buy into it. Not all of that packaging is designed to help you. You need to protect your-self from false advertising because it is thrown at you every day and can put your mind into a serious battle.

Let's take a brief look at some of the ways this happens through media.

- **Ads**—Buy Me! Buy Me! Buy Me! You know, the ads and commercials that make you feel like you just don't have the latest, greatest, and coolest stuff out there. They are designed to make you feel that if you just have their product, you'll be smarter, more popular and have more fun. And most of the time, these promises are empty promises. Be careful when you see ads for products that are supposed to make you look better and be happier. A product can't bring you joy. One single product can't make you look like a beauty queen—no matter what the ad says.

- **Music Lyrics**—Some music gives you a great beat, but a poisonous message is wrapped up in it. Before you know it, you're repeating messages that you don't really believe in. But the beat is great. It's a trick. Be very careful of what you

listen to and repeat—
even when the beat
makes you move. If
you keep repeat-
ing these messages,
you may begin
to believe them.
And that is why
Christian music
is a good choice.
To repeat over and
over the gospel
message—
the love of
Christ—can

actually help keep your mind in the right place,
regardless of what the beat sounds like.

■ **Web Ads**—Now you can hardly get away from
ads wherever you go. You have to deal with pop-
ups that come onto your screen from all over
the world. The good news and the bad news is
that you can now get more information than
any kid before you has ever been able to get. But
that means you need to protect your mind even
more so.

So how do you protect your mind from the overload?

You go back to the checklist we included in this chapter. Start at the beginning, and go through it until your heart and mind feel safe again. Stay in shape, and you won't be led off the path. You can do it!

Chapter 5

What Are You Thinking?

W hat do you spend most of your time thinking about? Do you ever think about what you're thinking about? That might sound like an odd question, but it's an important idea. Here's why.

Taming the Traveling Mind

Believe it or not, your mind goes off on its own, and before you know it, it can be thinking about the strangest things. Why, with no reason at all, my mind can easily start thinking about things like chocolate and ice cream and what I'd like to be doing. I can think about all sorts of things other than what I'm supposed to be doing. That can happen so easily when you're reading a book. Your mind can be on other things, and you don't even know what you've read. Maybe that even happens to you sometimes when you're reading the Bible.

Help from the Bible

Well, speaking of the Bible, we've been given a few hints in God's Word as to what our minds should be thinking. Let's look at a few of them so that when your mind is wandering off you can pull it back in.

If you look into the Word of God, especially at Psalm 119, you get one idea of what to think about. Starting at verse 9, the psalmist says:

How can a young person live a pure life? By obeying your word. With all my heart I try to obey you. Don't let me break your commands. I have taken your words to heart so I would not sin against you. Lord, you should be praised. Teach me your demands. My lips will tell about all the laws you have spoken. I enjoy living by your rules as people enjoy great riches. I think about your orders and study your ways. I enjoy obeying your demands, and I will not forget your word. (verses 9–16)

Let's take this Scripture apart and look at it more closely. The first question is asking, "How can a young person live a pure life?" (verse 9). That's a good question; in fact, it's a great question, and the answer comes right away.

How Can a Young Person Live a Pure Life?

"By obeying your word" (verse 9). By obeying God's Word! Wow!

There it is, and it sounds simple enough, but it would be helpful to give you a quick example of what it means to obey. Your mom or dad asks you to take out the trash and you do it. What you've basically done is "obey" them, which means you've done exactly what they asked you to do.

What If You Try and Fail?

But right away the Scripture identifies the problem. It says, "With all my heart I try to obey you" (verse 10). Isn't that the truth? Think about how hard you try to obey your parents and to live by the rules of your family. It's not always easy, is it? Sometimes you can't even do it. You may not have a rulebook to help you know all of the house rules, but you've got one when it comes to God's rules. Your Bible is right there for you to open anytime. Right?

You Ask God to Help You

Then the Scripture says, "Don't let me break your commands" (verse 10). Right away, it tells us that it's not easy to keep the rules, and we are going to need help. We want to obey, but it's hard. Then the Scripture explains, "I have taken your words to heart so I would not sin against you" (verse 11).

Now, I call that thinking about what you're thinking about. What does it mean when you say you've taken someone's words to heart? When your mom tells you how smart you are, how much she believes in you, and how much she loves you, those are words you can take to heart. When you take those words to heart, you feel good. You know some important things about yourself. You know you're loved because you're a special person—both to God *and* your family!

When You Take God's Word to Heart

When you take God's Word to heart, you understand that He loves you, He wants you to believe in what He has designed you to become, and He knows you're able to learn more about Him. And when you know that, it makes you want to work hard at becoming all that God wants you to become.

The Scripture continues with the phrase, "My lips will tell about all the laws you have spoken" (verse 13).

How Do You Show God You're Happy to Be His Kid?

Well, isn't that what you do when you're excited about something and you are happy? Don't you just want everybody to know what you know? Isn't that one of the ways you get great joy out of the love God has for you? You tell your friends. You tell almost anybody who will listen to you.

Finding Joy in "The Rules"

The Scripture says something else that's you don't want to miss. It says, "I enjoy living by your rules as people enjoy great riches" (verse 14). Whew! Do you want to read that again? Can you imagine telling your mom how much you enjoy living by her rules or the house rules? Most kids, no matter what age, aren't too thrilled when there are rules to follow. The writer of this Scripture not only loves the rules, but he loves them as much as some people enjoy being rich. Wow! Now, that's quite a mouthful. Think about that for a few moments.

Here's an Action You Can Take

Verses 15 and 16 of Psalm 119 end with an action, and it's one you can do, too. He says, "I think about your orders and study your ways. I enjoy obeying your demands and I will not forget your word."

This is the heart of thinking about what you're thinking about. Think about God's commands, study them, enjoy obeying them, and don't forget them.

That's big! Read it again:

■ Think about God's commands.
■ Study them.
■ Obey them.
■ Remember them.

It is important for you to think about what God has to say and what His rules are for your life. Thinking about what God wants you to know and understand takes a lot of time and a lot of study. It's not something you can put off until tomorrow. It's something to begin to know now, so that as you grow, God can add to your thoughts and your understanding to help you and to protect you out in the world.

A Couple of Stories You Already Know about Learning to Obey

More than a Whale's Tale...Our Man, Jonah!

You may have already heard of the story of Jonah. It's a good one for learning to obey God.

Here's the scene: The Lord spoke to Jonah and gave him specific instructions to go to Nineveh and preach against it because the people were being downright wicked and evil (see Jonah 1:1–2).

What did Jonah do? Well, he got right up and took off in the opposite direction. For some reason, Jonah had the crazy notion that God couldn't tell where he was if he was running, so he boughtt a ticket on a ship and headed for a city called Tarshish (verse 3).

Imagine Jonah slipping onto the deck of that ship and thinking that he had outwitted the God of the universe! Of course, we think this way, too, sometimes, so we can't be too hard on Jonah.

Anyway, after Jonah found a bunk in the bottom of the ship and fell asleep, God began to create a storm that nearly shook the ship apart. All the people on the ship were praying to any god they could think of for help, but nothing seemed to be changing the climate. Finally, they drew straws to figure out who was at fault, and you guessed it, every straw said it was Jonah (verses 4–7).

The crew members asked him who he was and where he was going. Jonah had to confess that he had run away from the God of the universe. Since the sea didn't get any calmer, Jonah told them to throw him into the water, and then the sea would calm down. The men tried to be kind to him and hoped they could just row their ship back to the shore, but the seas would not quiet down. They finally begged God's forgiveness because they didn't want to kill Jonah, but they had no choice but to throw him into the sea. As soon as they did, the seas calmed down (verses 8–15).

Swooped Up by a Big Fish

God caused a big fish to come along and swallow Jonah, and he lived inside the fish for three days and three nights (verse 17). When you're inside the belly of a fish, you start thinking a lot about what you're doing, and that's exactly what Jonah did. He prayed. He begged for forgiveness. He thanked God for being with him even in that situation. He made a promise to obey God forever. So God spoke to the fish and had the fish throw up Jonah back onto the dry land (see Jonah 3).

Coming Up for Air

Jonah must have been one great preacher for God to give him another chance to go and do what He wanted. Jonah didn't even have to prepare a message because God told him He would tell him what to say when he got there. So, the Bible says, Jonah obeyed (see 3:1–3).

Jonah walked partway through the city of Nineveh and told the people that after forty days the city would be destroyed (see 3:4). A very interesting thing happened, though, and Jonah didn't expect it.

The people believed God! They decided to stop eating and fast and wear clothes to show their sadness at how they had acted. Even the king of Nineveh did this. He commanded everyone to cry out to God for forgiveness. God then did a wonderful thing. He changed His mind. He did not destroy the city (see 3:5–10).

Jonah got mad. The funny thing is that Jonah was mad at God for forgiving the people of the city. He questioned God about being so willing to forgive them when they had been rotten people just a few days before. God was *very* patient with Jonah and gave him another example (see Jonah 4:1–4).

He made a plant grow to give Jonah shade when the sun was very hot. Jonah was pleased to sit by the plant and enjoy its shade. The next day, though, God caused a worm to eat the plant and make it die. Then Jonah suffered in the blazing heat (see 4:6–8).

Jonah was angry because the plant died. But God used the plant to teach Jonah a lesson. God asked Jonah why he was so angry that the plant died, when he hadn't done anything to make it grow. God told Jonah that just like he was concerned about the plant, God was concerned about the people of Ninevah, whom He had created. God wanted Jonah to preach to the people of Ninevah because God was concerned about them. (see 4:10–11).

Isn't it good to obey God? When you're thinking about the Word of God and how it can help you want to obey Him, remember Jonah. Jonah learned the hard way that disobedience is never good. We should be quick to follow God's Word.

Another Tale of Obedience

If You Can't Take the Heat, Stay Out of the Furnace

Another story about obedience is found in the book of Daniel. It's about three guys named Shadrach, Meshach, and Abednego. They were appointed by King Nebuchadnezzar to be leaders over Babylon. They were friends of Daniel, who helped the king interpret his dreams (see Daniel 1–2).

Though the king believed somewhat in the God of Daniel, he wasn't totally sold on Him just yet. In fact, King Nebuchadnezzar had a great big statue made out of gold that was ninety feet high, and he had set it up in a pretty clear place in Babylon for everyone to see (see Daniel 3:1). He was so pleased with this work that he sent out his royal messengers to tell people this news: "Anyone who doesn't bow down and worship will immediately be thrown into a blazing furnace" (Daniel 3:6).

Bowing to Gold Statues

Now that was serious, and people everywhere were falling to their knees. Some Babylonians, who were kind of gossipy and had a grudge against Shadrach, Meshach, and Abednego, wanted to make trouble.

They told the king that some of his very own men weren't playing according to the rules. They made the king agree to punish his own leaders (see 3:8–12).

Another Chance?

Because King Nebuchadnezzar really liked these three guys, he tried to give them another chance. He begged them to bow down to the statue and then they could all go home. The king was sure that no god could save them from the fiery furnace, and he figured they would just have to do what he asked (see 3: 13–15).

Things Heat Up

However, they answered like this because they were all about obeying God: "Nebuchadnezzar, we do not need to defend ourselves to you. If you throw us into the blazing furnace, the God we serve is able to save us from the furnace. He will save us from your power, O king. But even if God does not save us, we want you, O king, to know this: We will not serve your gods or worship the gold statue you have set up" (Daniel 3:16–18).

Well, that was hard for the king to hear, and he got very mad, and because of it, he told the furnace fire-builders to increase the heat by seven times the normal heat. He had his soldiers tie up Shadrach, Meshach, and Abednego and throw them into the furnace. The flames were so hot, the men who threw them into the furnace were killed instantly (see 3: 19–22).

The King's Surprise

After the three men had been dropped into the furnace, the king looked in to see how things were going. To his surprise, the three men were no longer tied up, and a fourth man was with them. They all looked fine. The king went to the opening of the furnace and called the men to come out (see 3:23–26).

Not Even Lightly Toasted

The three men came out. Their clothes weren't burned, their hair wasn't burned; why, they didn't even smell like smoke! Now what's up with that? The king became excited and started praising God. He was awed that the three men had obeyed their God, disobeyed him, and their lives had been spared. He did the best thing a king could do then—he promoted the three men to even higher positions in his kingdom (see 3:26–30).

What Can We Get from This Story?

Most of the time, if we don't obey God, it won't be a life-or-death matter. When you obey God, you know in your heart of hearts that you feel blessed and good and you understand what a special relationship you have. When you don't obey God, you want to hide like Jonah. In other words, obeying God brings a better life for you.

Getting back to thinking about what you're thinking about, then, these stories also show this. Jonah thought he had a better idea than God, and even after he ran away and God saved him, he still argued with God's decision in the end. If you think about that, you might decide that it's a better idea to do what God asks you to do right up front before you have to deal with the consequences.

Shadrach, Meshach, and Abednego help you to see that even when things seem hopeless, if you can keep trusting God to help you and believe that He will help you, your beliefs and thoughts will prevail. You could never stand up and state your beliefs as clearly as they did, if your thoughts had not been focused on those truths for a long time. These were men who lived according to God's will and purpose.

Back to Studying the Word

You'll get from your own study of the Word whatever you put into it. The more you study, the more you'll understand. The more you understand, the more power you'll have to face the tests and problems of the world.

The basic idea is that if you want to do what the Word of God says, you must spend time thinking about it. Romans 12:2 puts it like this: "Do not change yourselves to be like the people of this world, but be changed within by a new way of thinking. Then you will be able to decide what God wants for you; you will know what is good and pleasing to him and what is perfect."

Keep your eyes on the goal!

Chapter 6

Who's Minding Your Mind?

When you exercise, you get more out of it if you put your entire body, mind, and your spirit into it. If you have played any kind of sport, or practiced for anything from a school play to a piano recital, you know that you have to fully pay attention to what you're doing.

Learning about God and thinking about your life is

the same deal. You have to pay attention. You have to mind your mind and get it prepared to do your best. If you think you're going to play well while you're practicing for a recital, chances are you will. But if your mind isn't on practicing or playing, you probably won't do very well. You have to practice and practice and prepare for the big moments when you'll have to apply it. God is busy giving you tools to build you up and prepare you to be on His team. Let's look at some of the things that might keep your mind off the goal and distract you from the game.

Figuring Out If Your Thoughts Are Okay

One of the writers of the Bible was a follower of Jesus, and his name was Paul. He talked about having the "eyes of our hearts" opened and filled with light (see Ephesians 1:8 NLT).

Of course, you may remember that Paul was the guy who was against the followers of Jesus at the beginning. He was eager to destroy those who believed in God, and as he headed to a city called Damascus to find people to punish for their beliefs, he had an amazing experience. It went something like this (see Acts 9: 1–2)...

Paul and a group of his men were heading down the road toward the city in the early evening. Suddenly a very bright light beamed down on him from above, and a voice called out to him. "Why are you persecuting Me?" (see Acts 9:3–4).

Paul could hear the voice, but he couldn't see who was speaking to him because the light was so bright. He said, "Who are you?" (see verse 5).

Jesus answered him and told him who He was. He directed Paul to keep going into the city where he would be told what to do. When the beaming light disappeared, Paul discovered he was blind. His men had to help him go into the city (see verses 5–8).

Blind Eyes of the Heart

Before we go on and learn more of what happened to Paul, let's think about you and me. Are we ever blind to what God wants? Do we need a beam of light to shine on us so that we get what God wants us to know? Sometimes we are blind. Sometimes we can't see to save ourselves.

Think about what it means when you can't see. You know how it is when you're looking for the match to one of your socks, or one of your favorite shirts, and you know right where you put it but can't see it?

Finally, you ask your mom if she knows where it is, and it's so maddening because she always does, and you just don't know how she does it.

Not finding your sock is one kind of blindness, but not having the eyes of your heart open, well, that's another. You can always get another pair of socks. You can't get another heart, and you can't get another mind to try to understand what God wants you to know. You have to be willing to look and discover those for yourself. You have to search as though your life depended on it, because it does. Your spiritual life is that important to God.

So let's get back and find out what happened to Paul.

Let There Be Light...in Paul's Eyes!

Now you can imagine that Paul was freaked out by what had happened to him on that road. One minute he's a man with a mission, heading down a road, ready to bash a few Christians. The next minute, he's caught in a major light beam from the sky, knocked to the ground, hears a voice identifying Himself as Jesus, and when the light goes away, his sight goes away, too, and he's suddenly in the dark about what just happened.

When you're in the dark, you look to find the light switch as quickly as possible, and you can be sure Paul was hoping for something like that, too. When Paul got to Damascus, he stayed three days in the dark, praying and waiting for something to happen.

Meanwhile...on the Other Side of Town...

On the other side of town, God was busy preparing the answer to Paul's prayers to restore his sight. God had already talked to one of His servants, a guy named Ananias. God told Ananias that he needed to go visit

Paul (who at that point was still named Saul, but God was about to change his name, as well as his mission) and heal his blindness (see Acts 9:10–12).

Now that might sound like a nice thing for God to ask you to do. However, Ananias had to have some special "eyes of the heart" to understand why God would ask this of him. He had heard about Paul's reputation for doing nasty things to Christians. And he must have been nervous to meet Paul (see Acts 9:13–14).

God reassured Ananias that it would all be okay because He had some new plans for Paul. So Ananias went (see Acts 9:15–17).

When Ananias found Paul, he told him that Jesus had sent him, and he even told Paul that he knew Jesus had appeared to Paul on the road. That had to make Paul pretty sure this guy knew what he was doing, because Paul hadn't told anybody what had happened to him (see Acts 9:17).

Ananias told Paul that God sent him to help Paul get his sight back and to fill him with the Holy Spirit. At the touch of Ananias, something like scales fell from Paul's eyes. He saw the light and got baptized (see Acts 9:18–19).

What Does Paul's Story Have to Do with You?

You can read Paul's story for yourself in the ninth chapter of Acts. His story is a great example of what it means to be blind. Paul was a smart man. He went to the best schools. He had money. He had power. If he lived today, he'd have the big house on the hill and all the latest tech gadgets. His friends would have said that he was really the guy to know. His future looked bright.

Little did he know how bright! The point is that you can have all of the best "things," or the nicest house on the block, or be the smartest kid in school , and still be blind. That's right. Your mind and spirit can still be disconnected. That's what Paul's story is about, and that's what your story is about. You need to connect the dots between all the stuff you've learned so far in school, and at home, and at church, and see if the eyes of your heart have been opened yet. You need to see if you get it.

Get what? Do you get that you are a

child of God, and that He has a purpose for your life and a mission just for you? Do you get that the sooner you start on it, the more you can do for Him and the more light he can shine on you and help you fight off any of the darkness that ever tries to get around you?

You need to see the light just like Paul did. You need to have ways for your mind, the part of you that is totally smart, to catch up with your spirit, the part of you that is totally owned by God. According to the Bible, the mind and the spirit have to work together to understand this completely.

How Can Your Mind Help Your Spirit?

First of all, you have to know that sometimes your spirit is really working hard to help you understand things about God. So even though the spirit is trying to help you live a better life, your mind can just be too busy to hear it and not catch on to what is happening.

Think of it like this. Think about that time your math teacher was trying to explain square roots and you were there listening, but your mind was off in a hundred other directions. Your mind was *too* busy to listen, and you didn't quite get the lesson on square roots.

Add to your wandering mind the fact that your

friend is trying to get your attention. Your best friend is across the room trying to whisper something to you and mouthing every syllable so that you can understand what is being said. But the whole room is in an uproar, and for some reason, everyone is talking at once and you can't hear your neighbor, much less your friend across the room. There's so much noise now, you can hardly hear yourself think.

If your mind is overloaded with thoughts of the day, with other kids' voices playing in your ears, along with what Mom said would be for dinner and what Dad said you should remember today, you're not going to be tuned in. In fact, it's amazing you can get your schoolwork done at all.

So How Do You Hear God's Voice?

You get very, very quiet. You take a deep breath and pray. You listen.

Your mind should be at peace. It should be ready to listen, be alert, and be at rest. Your mind cannot go wandering.

We've talked a bit already about how you can be aware of a mind that wanders off. One thing you have to do is concentrate. Remember the preparation we talked about at the beginning of the chapter; when you're preparing to run a race, or do some exercise, you've got to concentrate. You've got to focus on the job at hand. Your mind needs that kind of focus all the time.

If you didn't get enough sleep last night, or if you've got worries on your mind, you might have trouble with this idea of focus. If you're reading the same page in your history book for the third time, the chances are you're not able to focus. Rest a little, and then try to concentrate more later.

Everybody daydreams now and then. We're not really talking about when that happens, because sometimes it's important to just let your mind rest. We're talking about the fact that you can have some control over letting your mind wander off, and you can run after it and get it to come back before it gets too far away—especially when you need to pay attention to a lesson, sermon, or God.

If your dog wanders off into the neighborhood, you go calling for him to come home. You don't want him to stray too far from your house. The same is true for your thoughts. If your mind wanders off, you need to call it back home.

What Kinds of Things Distract Your Mind?

Most kids will say they can easily do their homework in front of the TV or on the bus ride home from school with fifty loud kids jumping around. They might even say they can have music going and a slice of pizza in hand and still get an A on the paper they're writing. That's what they say, at least. Maybe you're one of those who can do that. Maybe you're not. It's good to look at how easily you can be distracted, though, because maybe then you can stop those distractions right in their tracks.

See if you can put this list in the order of priority of what you find most distracting. Number from ten to one on a piece of paper, and see if you can figure out the number one thing that distracts you when you're trying to focus on something you need to do.

Common Distractions

- Commercials on TV.
- Songs on the radio or your device.

- Sister or brother who interrupts you.
- Notifications on your phone or tablet.
- Cat jumping in your lap.
- Somebody outside mowing the lawn.
- Fire engine screaming down the street.
- Barking dog.
- Hunger.
- Ringing doorbell.

Look at your list and the order you put it in, and you should have some idea of what you need to do to find a more peaceful place to work when you have to concentrate. Think about the times when you want to pray. Do any of these things distract you then? If you can name those things that keep you from letting your mind be at peace, then you can work on ways to keep them from distracting you. And once you do that, you'll have a weapon to help you battle the whole mind-wandering issue.

Are You Wondering?

Some of us never outgrow the "wonder" years. We wonder what will be for dinner. We wonder what the test will be like in English. We wonder if we'll have good friends all through life. We wonder if people really like us. We wonder if Mom or Dad will take us to the movies. We wonder about things all the time.

It's true, healthy curiosity can be a good thing! You can wonder about a variety of interesting topics and even start studying them. That kind of curiosity is what wondering should be all about. Most scientists start out by wondering about something.

But we're talking about a different kind of wondering here. We're talking about all those little things that keep your mind tied up, or occupied, because you can't really do anything about them or get the answers right away. They are simply not in your control. When your mind gets lost in that kind of wondering, it is a total waste of your time. You aren't going to get one answer anytime soon.

When Your Head Is Full of You!

When you're wondering about everything, you have a hard time making decisions, you feel confused, and you aren't able to hear anything God might be trying to tell you. Your head is too full of you! When your head vibrates with all the things you wonder about, it can't be calm enough to receive any guidance from the Holy Spirit. You need to stop all that wondering and calm your mind and pray. When you pray, you'll be able to get the answers you're seeking.

When you read what the Bible says in Mark 11: 23–24, you'll see that Jesus did not say to His followers, "Whatever you ask for in prayer, wonder if you will get it." Instead, He said, "Whatever you ask for in prayer, believe that you will receive it—and you will!"

You need to move from wondering to believing!

Chapter 7

Making the Grade Means Getting a New Mind

You work hard in school. You try to get the best grades possible by cramming your head full of ideas and facts and opinions. You do it in every class you take, and by the end of the day, your mind can be on overload. You might wonder if your brain will simply short-circuit.

As good as it is to get those A's and to learn all that

you can, sometimes it's even better for you to just take a break. Do a few somersaults, pop some popcorn, and rest. Go back to the beginning and take a deep breath. Going back to the beginning in this case means going back to your source of strength and inspiration and real knowledge. The truth is, the fact that God loves you and He wants to help you with everything you do in your life—including school—is the most important thing you need to know. And the best thing you can do is put on the mind of Christ.

Oh, sure, you're thinking. *That's not exactly easy. If that was a test, I'd probably fail.*

Well, you're right. It's not easy, but it is something you can study up on and work on. In fact, there's a lot you can do.

All through this book, we've been talking about how you can make the kind of choices that will give you the right mind-set. Right choices lead to right thinking. Right thinking leads to Jesus. You've hung in there this far, so let's keep going, okay?

How Do You Put on the Mind of Christ?

First Corinthians 2: 11–13 gives us part of the answer when it says: "No one knows the thoughts of God except the Spirit of God. Now we did not receive the spirit of the world, but we received the Spirit that is from God so that we can know all that God has given us. And we speak about these things, not with words taught us by human wisdom but with words taught us by the Spirit."

Wow! What does that mean? It means that once we believe in Jesus, God gives us the Holy Spirit to come into our hearts and minds and help us understand more fully the things of God. If we didn't have Jesus, we wouldn't be able to understand the things of the Spirit.

As we grow, we learn more from the Spirit, and we become more like Jesus. At least, that's the goal. Sure, it sounds easy enough, but let's keep going.

What Does It Mean to Really Put on the Mind of Christ?

Okay, I've brought the question back up again because the Bible verse told us what happens when we have the Holy Spirit to help us understand the things of God and the ways that Jesus might think. But how do we really do that?

First of all, we don't get a quick zap and suddenly our minds are transformed into focusing on the right thoughts. That would be nice, but it's not going to happen. We also don't get to drop a packet of good thoughts into some water, watch them fizz, drink them down, and suddenly be transformed. In fact, we don't get this mind of Christ quickly and easily at all. It's a lifelong process from being a kid to being an adult and having a mind that wants to keep learning and growing. All of us are working on it. All of us want to get more of what Jesus thinks and less of what we think.

Part of having a change of mind is about having a change of heart. When your heart is "in the right place," as we so often say, then you're more apt to do the right things. Let's look at some more Bible verses that speak about how our minds work with our hearts.

Heart, Soul, and Mind

Jesus replied, "You must love the Lord your God with all your heart, all your soul, and all your mind" (Matthew 22:37 NLT). What does it take to do anything with your heart, and your soul, and your mind?

What is your heart? Your heart is your emotional center. It is the place where you feel deeply about the things that are important to you. It's the place where your mom and your dad and your family and friends live. It's the place where you have the deepest desires of what you want to become and what you want life to be about. You feel these things in your heart.

What is your soul? Your soul is the essence of you that will live forever. It is the place where the Spirit of God lives within your being and connects to all the other aspects of you that surrender to the will of God. John of the Cross said, "The soul is in itself a most lovely and perfect image of God."

In other words, it's worth understanding, and you'll understand more about your soul as you continue to grow in Jesus.

What is your mind? Your mind is the tool that God has created in you that gives you the power to think and react and look at life from all points of view. It is the keeper of your joy and your sorrow. It is the place where you get to know who you are and what you are to become. It is a part of your being that is continually in need of being renewed.

Now, put these three things together and add the idea of love. Love with all your heart, all your soul, and all your mind. Well, that's a pretty giant idea! If you think about loving your mom or someone else you care about with this degree of focus, you will begin to discover where we're going here.

But wait, we still have to add the most important ingredient for this statement. Who are you to love? You're to love *God* with all your heart, all your soul, and all your mind. Now try to imagine that!

The Things You Love

Think for a moment about the things you love. You love spaghetti, you love your dog, you love chocolate, you love music, and you love your best friend. Those things are pretty small in comparison to what Jesus is suggesting here. Those things we just named don't need all your heart and mind and soul. Only God needs that. We're looking at love in a whole new way. Maybe we could even guess that God wants you to love Him like this, because that's how He loves you!

Luke 10:27 puts it a little differently. It says:

Love the Lord your God with all your heart, all your soul, all your strength, and all your mind. Also, love your neighbor as you love yourself.

Luke even adds that you must love God with your physical body, as well, with "all your strength." Imagine having all this love for God and knowing that everything in you is tuned into this great love. What are you supposed to do with it?

One of the answers given is this: You are to "love your neighbor as you love yourself." If you love your neighbor as yourself, it's a pretty sure thing that you have tried to put on the mind of Christ. You have learned how important it is to love with everything you've got and to put the needs of others before yourself. That's the goal. That's what God wants you to do.

One More Time ... What Does It Mean to Love Your Neighbor?

You've been learning about loving your neighbor all your life. You learned to share your toys in nursery school. You learned to help out around the house and lend somebody a hand when you were needed. It's the same idea, except that it isn't a matter of doing it only when you feel like it. It's a matter of choosing that way of being and acting all the time. It's a matter of putting on the mind of Christ each day.

In Acts 2–4, the believers were getting their first experience of the Holy Spirit. This was a new thing for them, and something really important happened to them. They were in love with the Lord and had love for one another.

"All the believers were of one heart and mind, and they felt that what they owned was not their own; they shared everything they had" (Acts 4:32 NLT). That passage goes on to say that people who owned houses and property sold them, so that they could bring the money back and share it with all those in need (see verse 34). That's a powerful way to be of one heart and mind. Taking care of all those in need would be "putting on the mind of Christ." Wouldn't that be an amazing thing to see?

So How Can You Take Care of Your Neighbors?

- Ask if you can volunteer at church in the nursery or help the younger kids with a project.
- Help out with vacation Bible school.
- Research ways that kids can help in your local communities.
- Pray for others.
- Be a good citizen.
- Help out around the house.
- Hug the people in your family.
- Volunteer with your family at a soup kitchen.

- See what you can clean out of your closet and give to someone less fortunate.
- See if you have any old toys that you could give away—or even give away a new toy to someone who doesn't get new stuff often.
- Write notes to people you don't get to see often and let them know you care about them.
- Get a pen pal through your church, either in the United States or in another country.
- Ask your parents for some other ideas—and then do them together!

Be sure whatever you do, though, that you get your parents' permission before you start. These are just some ways that you can be a good neighbor and help others. I'm sure you know lots of other ways and that you're already sharing your special gifts. In those ways, you truly are "putting on the mind of Christ." You will find as you do for others your thinking about everything will be more in line with God's word.

Keeping a Positive Mind

Being a positive person is about having a positive mind-set, which is not the same as pretending to be happy all the time. Having a positive mind-set is really about how you choose to "see" the things that go on in your life. Let's look at an example.

Hurricane Closes the Disney Theme Park

Your family vacation has been set for months, and you're all heading for Disney World. You've been counting the days and saving your pennies and figuring out what you'll wear and what you'll say when you meet Mickey and Minnie. You're set to go! The day before you're supposed to take off, Hurricane Ruin Everything comes through, and the park is forced to close. According to the news, it will be closed for several days for repairs after the hurricane leaves the area. Your family will be given rain checks to come again whenever they choose.

What Will You Do When This Happens?

Whether you have a positive or a negative mind-set, you are expected to be disappointed about this. After all, you were looking forward to really having fun and getting away from your normal routine. No doubt, your parents are upset, too. That's a normal reaction.

But what you do with your disappointment after you've gotten through those first feelings of anger and sadness is the key. Let's look at some possible reactions. Take a look at what our friends Sulky, Zippy, and Sassy would do.

Sulky's Story

Why did that old hurricane have to come now? Why couldn't it ruin everything for somebody else? Why

did it have to ruin the one fun thing I was going to get
to do this whole year?!

Everything bad happens to me. My friends are
already gone on their vacations, and now I don't have
anyone to play with. Mom made me clean my room
every day for weeks because we were going on this
trip, and now we're not even going. I just hate my life.
How come nothing good ever happens to me?

As you can see, Sulky took the whole incident and
turned it into a personal defeat. Somehow, the whole
world is down on Sulky, and this hurricane was part of
some kind of plot to make his life miserable. Clearly,
he's not meant to enjoy life, and everything is ruined.
That's his mind-set. Is it doing him any good? Do you
think his life is really that awful?

Zippy's Story

Zippy was really disappointed when she heard that
her family would not be able to make the trip to Flor-
ida. She looked at her packed bags and her pictures
of Cinderella and all the characters she was looking
forward to seeing and thought about what to do.

She looked through her book about all the things
you could see and do at Disney World and had an
idea. She'd make everybody in her family a special

pass for getting into the park. It would be a "hurricane can't stop us" pass, and they could pretend they were playing in the park that very evening. After all, it would just be a few weeks before they would get to go for real.

Zippy started working. She cut out pictures of rides and space stations and animals and characters and put them on pieces of cardboard. Then she put the name of each person in her family next to one of the pieces. She created a special invitation for each one to imagine what was going on there and to talk about the fun they would have in a few weeks when the park was open again.

Zippy took her work downstairs to share with her family. They all had fun as they talked about what they would do when they actually got to the park. Zippy helped her whole family feel better, and they stayed up late playing games.

After all, the hurricane wasn't anybody's fault. Zippy wanted to help everyone feel better as soon as possible. What a difference a positive attitude makes!

Sassy's Story

Sassy didn't take the news of the hurricane well. She started out sulking a bit, but then she just got angry.

Her anger made her feel worse and worse, and she took it out on everybody in the house.

"I don't believe the news," she told her dad. "I think we should just go anyway. It's probably not that bad."

"Planes can't even fly into the area right now, Sassy," her dad explained. "They really are having a hurricane. Don't worry, we'll still go in a few weeks when things get back to normal."

Sassy blew up. She stormed up the stairs, slammed her bedroom door, and started throwing things around in her room. Her mom came in to check on her, and Sassy just yelled at her at the top of her lungs. She didn't care what anyone had to say. She was angry, and she wanted them all to know it.

Sassy even shouted at the cat, who *really* didn't have anything to do with it!

It's pretty clear by these three examples what a difference a positive mind-set can make. No matter what comes your way to disappoint you—and disappointment will come your way a lot in life—you have to manage it. You have to create a way to think about it that makes it better and not worse. That's called putting things into perspective. You choose to look at your situation in a positive manner rather in a negative way. It's your choice, and it can make all of the difference in your life.

How? Think Positive Thoughts

Since you're already aware of "putting on the mind of Christ," you have some idea of what it might mean to think in a positive way. You know for sure that God is positive. You know that partly because you learned from the time you were a little kid that God is love. Love is positive. You get the picture.

What can you do to add a positive spin to the things that happen in your life? You can:

- Look for the good in any situation.
- Remember that you can change your mind and your attitude.
- Ask God for help.
- Look for something better to come along. Know that God wants what is best for you.
- Know that God cares when you're disappointed.
- Look for ways to solve a problem rather than add to it.
- Let people you love help you.
- Help people you love.
- Eat pizza.
- Keep a journal so that you can remember what you did that was helpful in case this ever happens again.
- Choose to make the best of things.
- Add your own ideas.

You can see that even though you may not be able to control the weather or hurricanes or even smaller events in your life, you can control how you choose to look at them. Asking yourself how Jesus would handle the situation is a good place to start. You can always be a bright spot if you choose to be positive in the storms that come along in your life.

You see, every time something blows in on you, you can always go back to the beginning, the place where Jesus will meet you and help you get through what's ahead. You never have to face life's challenges alone. That's good news!

Chapter 8

Doubt and Depression Belong in the Dumpster

Two of the biggest battles that your mind will ever face are feelings of doubt and depression. Both of them will slink around you, waiting for a chance to break into your mind and make you believe all kinds of things that just aren't true. Think of them both as big, dumb thugs who have no business being in your life. They never are part of God's plan for you, and they will have a hard time ever bothering you if you have put on the mind of Christ.

So How Do You Battle Feelings of Doubt?

You can start by writing this little poem on a piece of paper and hanging it on your wall.

> *Doubt sees the obstacles,*
> *Faith sees the way;*
> *Doubt sees the blackest night,*
> *Faith sees the day;*
> *Doubt dreads to take a step,*
> *Faith soars on high; Doubt questions, "Who believes?"*
> *Faith answers, "I"*
>
> *—(believed to have been written by William*
> *(Harvey) Jett*

I don't believe that God ever puts doubt in our minds. Romans 12:3 says, "Do not think you are better than you are. You must decide who you really are by the amount of faith God has given you." Earlier in the chapter, Paul wrote: "Don't copy the behavior and customs of this world, but let God transform you into a new person by changing the way you think" (verse 2 NLT).

So, the question is, will you let God transform your thinking, or will you let the feeling of doubt tell you what you can and cannot do? This is a great thing to learn now, because it will help you all your life. Doubt is not from God.

The funny part is this: Feelings of doubt try to trip you up because you have faith. If you didn't have faith, they'd probably leave you alone. It's your faith they try to attack. God put the faith in your heart. Don't let anything or anyone take it away!

How Can You Battle Against Doubt?

Read, Study, and Speak the Word

Feelings of doubt can creep up any time you're tired or worried or simply not at your best. Usually your spirits are low when they come. The best thing you can do is be well armed with the Word. You need to have some great Bible verses to throw back in

Doubt's face, and before long Doubt will get tired of bothering you and go away.

If you know the Word, you can recognize when Doubt is ringing your doorbell and send faith to answer. Doubt fills your head with lies because he wants to make you think your faith in Jesus is not enough. You know better, though!

One of my favorite stories, when I'm starting to feel doubt sneak up on me, is the one in Romans 4. It's the story of what happened to Abraham way back in Genesis. Let's look at Abraham's faith and see how that might help us, too.

Abraham's Story

Keep in mind that I'm going to tell you this story in my own words, but you can read the actual account yourself in Romans 4.

Abraham Believed God

The story starts out with this simple statement: Abraham believed God (see Romans 4:3). God was so delighted about that that He gave Abraham some special privileges. Now, just so you're clear about this, Abraham didn't do a lot of great things. He didn't do so many good deeds that God picked him out of a crowd. Therefore, Abraham couldn't really brag about what he did to get God's special blessings. No, Abraham simply believed God.

God liked hanging out with Abraham because of Abraham's faith, not his works. So how did this faith stuff help Abraham?

It meant that Abraham had a relationship with God that was based on things of the heart, soul, and mind. Those are the things we talked about before and the ones that Jesus told us were important to have. Abraham had that very kind of love for God.

The Bible reminds us that faith is the key. God's promise is given to us as a free gift. What was it Abraham had that maintained his faith? What was the promise God made to him?

The Father of Many Nations

Abraham believed God when God told him that he would have a lot of children (see Romans 4:17). He even said that Abraham's children would be as numerous as the stars (verse 18). That had to sound pretty impossible to Abraham. However, Abraham believed that it could happen, even though he was technically too old to be a father. He was already one hundred years old. (And you think your dad is old!) Sarah, his wife, was also very old. She was older than women normally are when they have children, yet Abraham believed God could do anything (verse 19). If God said he'd have children, then he was pretty sure he would have children (verses 20–21).

Abraham was totally convinced that God could fulfill His promise. Even though Sarah was a little less certain, she remained faithful to her husband. Her husband remained faithful to God, and before the whole thing was over, Isaac was born.

Why This Is a Good Story

I like this story a lot because it reminds me that all things are possible with God. Some things may seem too hard if you don't let God in, but if you do, He can bring about anything that is right for you. This is a great story of what it means not to doubt God. It shows us how faith and belief in what God says will help us beat doubt every time.

Let's take a look at another story in the Bible about a man known as Thomas, the Doubter.

Thomas, the Doubter

Shortly after Jesus died and rose from the grave, there was a disciple who needed more proof. Chances are that some of us would need the same proof to believe.

Mary was the first to encounter Jesus after the resurrection. She was the one who told the story of her conversation with Him. Shortly after that, Jesus appeared to His disciples, but Thomas was not present at that meeting. When Thomas came in and they told him the story, Thomas said he could not believe unless he saw the nail wounds in Jesus' hands and the wound in His side. Here's what John 20:26–29 has to say:

> *Eight days later the disciples were together again, and this time Thomas was with them. The doors were locked; but suddenly, as before, Jesus was standing among them. He said, "Peace be with you." Then he said to Thomas, "Put your finger here and see my hands. Put your hand into the wound in my side. Don't be faithless any longer. Believe!"*
>
> *"My Lord and my God!" Thomas exclaimed. Then Jesus told him, "You believe because you have seen me. Blessed are those who haven't seen me and believe anyway." (John 20:26–29 NLT)*

Perhaps the old saying, "Seeing is believing," comes from this very story. Questions will arise often in your walk of faith. Feelings of doubt will come around and attack you any chance they get.

What will your answer be? Will you believe anyway?

Now, Let's Take a Look at the Feeling of Depression

I sincerely hope that you haven't had to deal with depression yet in your young life. And I pray that you never will. Chances are, though, that you'll be around someone who suffers from depression at some time or other. How does depression happen, and how does it take over? How can you overcome it?

When nothing ever seems to go right for you and you're feeling tired and icky all the time, it might be a bit of depression.

Depression can make you feel like the weight of the world is on your shoulders, and you don't have answers for anything. The sun goes out, nobody's playing anymore, and everything is gloomy.

In my book for adults, I walk through Psalm 143 to demonstrate some ways to help overcome feelings of depression. We'll use a different Bible translation for you, but let's go through this psalm and see how it can help.

Getting Back to the Light

Step One: Figure Out What Is Causing the Problem

My enemy has chased me. He has knocked me to the ground. He forces me to live in darkness like those in the grave. Psalm 143:3 NLT

What's the problem? The writer of this psalm was being attacked by the forces of darkness. He was feeling like everything around him was black, and he had no control over what was happening.

When you have a problem and you can't figure out

where it is coming from or why you feel so blue, you might want to stop and see if you could be in the middle of a spiritual battle. The battle is going on all the time, and sometimes it can affect you personally.

Step Two: See What the Feeling of Depression Is Really Doing to You

I am losing all hope; I am paralyzed with fear.
                                    Psalm 143:4 NLT

Your response to depression is to become fearful and hopeless. You begin to believe that you're simply in the dark and that you can't find your way back to the light.

Step Three: Think About the Things That Make You Feel Good

I remember the days of old. I ponder all your great works. I think about what you have done.
                                    Psalm 143:5 NLT

It may help you to stop if you can and think about the good things God has done for you so far. Think about the loving family He has given you or the good friends you have. Think about the vacation you took last year or the fun you had in summer camp. Think about the good things.

Step Four: Thank the Lord Anyway!

I reach out for you. I thirst for you as parched land thirsts for rain.

Psalm 143:6 NLT

What happens when you're feeling down? You want to get things to feel better. You feel dry and thirsty, and you want to have someone take care of you. The writer of this Scripture says that one choice you have is to "reach out" for the Lord. Look to Him to help you to keep believing that He has the answers. Believe that He can fill you up and make you happy again. You can begin that step by thanking Him for all He's done for you in the past.

Remember that Jesus said that He is "living water" (see John 4:10).

Step Five: Ask God to Help You!

Come quickly, Lord, and answer me, for my depression deepens. Don't turn away from me, or I will die.

Psalm 143:7 NLT

You see what is happening. You feel like you can't hold on much longer, and you really need help. You're like a person hanging on to a rope for dear life and hoping someone gets there in time.

When you call on God for help, His rescue arrives instantly! He sends the Holy Spirit to comfort and care for you and strengthen you so that you can hold on until things turn around.

Step Six: Listen to What God Wants to Tell You

Let me hear of your unfailing love to me in the morning, for I am trusting you. Show me where to walk, for I have come to you in prayer.

Psalm 143:8 NLT

Look at what this is telling you. It says three very important things:

1. You must want more than anything to hear what God would say to you. Your love for Him must be your guide.
2. You must trust God to pull you through.
3. You must ask Him to guide your steps and give you direction, because that is your prayer.

Step Seven: You Must Pray and Pray Some More

Save me from my enemies, Lord; I run to you to hide me.

Psalm 143:9 NLT

Look at where the writer of this Scripture is putting all of his attention. He is asking God to save him. He is telling the Lord that he wants to be even closer to Him. Imagine a baby chick running to a mother hen, getting shelter under her wing because he's afraid of something in the barnyard.

That's the picture. You can go to the Lord for shelter, and He will protect you. You must keep your eyes on Him as the One who can really help you, and take your eyes off the problem.

Step Eight: Ask God for Wisdom and Guidance

Teach me to do your will, for you are my God. May your gracious Spirit lead me forward on a firm footing.
Psalm 143:10 NLT

How many times do we lose our way? How many times do we put all of our worry and energy into the problem, instead of asking God for help?

The writer is not only asking God for help, he's saying, "I still need more lessons in doing Your will. I'm still a student. I'm still in need of a teacher. Help me to do Your will because You are my God, You are my personal Savior. I've already committed my heart and mind to You."

Then he ends with a wish, a sort of prayer. He prays

that God's gracious Spirit will lead him forward. He says, "Put me on steady ground, Lord. Keep me safe in You. Help me to land on my feet."

If you have the feeling of depression at your back door, you can keep it away with these steps. If you need help, have your mom or dad or a good friend work through the steps with you. That's why God gave us people to be around us and care for us.

The main thing to remember is that you do have some choices in how you think about things. You have some tools that you can use to help you think better, but these tools will not wipe away all your troubles. If

they did, they'd be magic formulas needing a wand, not real-life issues needing the grace of a heavenly Father. You are a child of God. You always have a place to share your troubles. God will always choose to help you through until you can see the light again.

Chapter 9

Weeds of Worry (and How to Get Rid of Them!)

L et's say God planted you in a garden. You started as a small seed, and He nourished you and gave you just enough to drink and just enough to eat. He brought the sun out so that you could grow and enjoy the beauty all around you. And then you *really*

grew up. Now that you're fully in bloom, you can see the world even better than when you were tiny. Now you start to worry about everything.

Come to think of it, God did plant the first people in a Garden, and He did just that: He provided everything for them. He gave them all they needed to grow strong and be happy. He was always there for them and loved to watch them enjoy their beautiful surroundings. Then, one day, they, too, started to worry. Let's go visit Adam and Eve, our first parents, back in Paradise. That's where the worry all began.

Planting Worries in the Garden

Genesis 3 gives us the story.

Now the snake was the most clever of all the wild animals the Lord God had made. One day the snake said to the woman, "Did God really say that you must not eat fruit from any tree in the garden?"

The woman answered the snake, "We may eat fruit from the trees in the garden. But God told us, 'You must not eat fruit from the tree that is in the middle of the garden. You must not even touch it, or you will die.'"

But the snake said to the woman, "You will not die. God knows that if you eat the fruit from that tree, you will learn about good and evil and you will be like God."

The woman saw that the tree was beautiful, that its fruit was good to eat, and that it would make her wise. So she took some of its fruit and ate it. She also gave some of the fruit to her husband, and he ate it.

Then, it was as if their eyes were opened. (Genesis 3:1–7)

Never Listen to a Snake!

The same snake that tricked Eve in the Garden tries to trick you, too.

Do you see what he did in the Garden? First, he questioned Eve as though she didn't really understand what God was saying. He acted like he was just asking an innocent question. He caused her to doubt what she knew. He caused her to even doubt what she was told by God Himself.

Step Back!

Step back a moment and think about times when you've started to doubt. Maybe someone teased you about your faith, or they asked a question that you didn't have an answer to, and so you started to wonder if you actually knew God as much as you thought you did. Well, that's kind of what happened to Eve. She started to doubt that she really knew what she should do.

Now look at what that crafty snake does. He goes after Eve again. He tells her something that he knows will excite her interest. He tries to make himself seem like the one "who really knows the answers about God." His questions make Eve worry about the truth. The snake literally plays with her mind. And that's exactly how doubt works.

The Snake Pit

Going back to you: You may have had the experience of someone at school putting doubt in your mind about something you already believe. For example, one of your friends might tell you it's okay to use curse words when your mom isn't around. But you know it's not; that's not how a believer talks—whether your mom is around or not. But still, your friend keeps at you. Your friend starts cursing, and he seems cool, so you think you will try it, too. Before you know it, you're using curse words more and more. And the more you use these words, the less you sound like a Christian. There may be some kids who want to ask you questions about your faith, but your language turns them away.

Your light is not shining for Christ when you use bad language—all because you listened to a friend who put doubt in your mind about what you should do.

That's why you should never talk to a snake. A snake in any form is there to spread doubt and worry and trap you into sin. Why do you think a snake crawls on its belly? Why do you think it hides in the dark?

We could get more things from this story, but the main point I want you to see is how doubt and worry can work together to tempt you to sin, to go against the things that you know are good.

A Strong Foundation

You're never too young to learn how to stand firm in your beliefs. Your mind will be bombarded with lots of information, and it's up to you to decide if it is good or bad for you. If you don't have a solid foundation of God's Word, you may find yourself being bullied or pushed around by other people's ideas.

And before you

know it, if you don't know who you are in Christ, your foundation will start to show cracks of doubt and discontent. A good building is only as solid as its foundation, so you want to make it as strong as possible.

Finding the Peace Again

Peace of mind is essential to your growth and well-being. You may have noticed how often the Bible writers and disciples greeted each other with a wish for peace. They lived in hard times, and they didn't take for granted the glorious moments when their minds felt free and their hearts were at rest in God.

You shouldn't, either. We're fortunate to live in a culture that allows us freedom of worship and the opportunity to express our faith in God anytime and anyplace. Much of both the ancient world and the modern world is not that blessed. Peace is a gift of God and one of the benefits of having your heart and mind lined up with God's will.

Peace Is a Fruit of the Spirit

In Galatians 5:22–23, we read about the fruit of the Spirit. Let's look at these verses and see how they can help us when we have anxious or worried minds.

But the Spirit produces the fruit of love, joy, peace, patience, kindness, goodness, faithfulness, gentleness, self-control...

This Scripture tells us that God's Spirit lives inside of us and that we have all the things listed above. However, *having* something and *using* something are two different things. You can be given a present, but if you don't open it, you can't use it. God's Word promises us His peace, but we have to do more than just talk about having it; we need to put it into use.

So, let's take some time to focus on peace. You can't have a worried mind and a peaceful mind at the same time. That just doesn't work! You have to choose. When you come across a tough situation, when something doesn't go your way at school, will you choose peace or worry? Sure, your first response may be to worry about it, but placing it in God's hands is trusting Him to take care of you and work everything out. He's a good Father and He wants to do just that!

The Problem with Worry

Think about it. Has worrying ever helped you before? Does it make your problem better, or does it just make you think about the problem more and what can happen?

Many times what you worry about is all in your mind—it never happens, or it doesn't happen the way you have thought about in your mind. So, basically, worrying is a big waste of time. It just makes you unhappy and afraid, instead of peaceful and positive.

When you think of all the time and energy worrying takes up, wouldn't you much rather you much rather spend that time praying and getting closer to God? When you pray, you get more peace and can live a happier life. That's much better than worrying.

So you get the point—worrying doesn't give you

any solutions. It doesn't ever take you to God. It just takes you deeper within yourself.

So What's Your Worry Anyway?

Let's look at some more examples in the Bible of things that cause us to worry. Isn't it interesting to see how current and relevant the Bible is? We can pull wonderful examples from it to help us with what's going on today in the twenty-first century. Amazing!

Starting with Matthew 6:25, we can see how useless it is to worry about the everyday things in our lives. Jesus says:

> So I tell you, don't worry about the food or drink you need to live, or about the clothes you need for your body. Life is more than food, and the body is more than clothes. Look at the birds in the air. They don't plant or harvest or store food in barns, but your heavenly Father feeds them. And you know that you are worth much more than the birds. You cannot add any time to your life by worrying about it.
>
> And why do you worry about clothes? Look at how the lilies in the field grow. They don't work or make clothes for themselves. But I tell you that even Solomon with his riches was not dressed as beautifully as one of these flowers.

*God clothes the grass in the field, which is alive
today but tomorrow is thrown into the fire. So you can
be even more sure that God will clothe you. Don't have
so little faith! (verses 25–30)*

Your Life Is More Important Than Things!

As you're learning to think about things in new ways,
I hope you'll discover that you're already pretty smart.
In fact, you may have already noticed that the closer
you stick to God, the less you have to worry. The
more you try to keep up with the world, the more you
can feel dissatisfied with what you have. The truth is
that whether or not you have the latest stuff—your
own cell phone or the trendiest clothes—you have
more than most of the kids in the world. In fact, just
having food on the table every day and a place to take
a shower when you want to or a cozy place to sleep
means you have more than most of the world.

So What If You Don't Have Everything You Want?

Have you ever felt like you don't have everything that
your best friend has? Stop and think about it. Even if

you didn't have all of those things, do you have air to breathe?

The Scripture you read just a minute ago is a reminder that God has taken care of all of the ones He created, right down to the birds and the flowers. He has made sure that every single thing is cared for and is meant to be enjoyed. Remember, having just the essentials (food, clothing, a place to live, running water) makes you very fortunate!

You might want to take some time and go watch a few birds. Do they look worried? G. K. Chesterton said that "angels can fly because they take themselves lightly." Sometimes it seems like we need to do that, too. We need to take ourselves lightly and take our faith seriously, and we'll know without a doubt or worry anywhere that everything we really need is taken care of; God has already planned for our good. He has already planned for your good.

In fact, He reminds you that you're worth even more than any bird! So, surely if God takes care of them, He will take care of you!

Seek, Look for, Go after, Pursue God!

One of the biggest things to remember any time you are tempted to worry is tied to this verse. It's from that same section of Matthew, verse 33. It says, "The thing you should want most is God's kingdom and doing what God wants. Then all these other things you need will be given to you."

In other words, when you're really looking for God to be number one in your life, and you look for Him in everything you do, and you fill your thoughts with Him, wanting more of what He has to offer, you'll discover that you are at peace. You will discover that you are being taken care of in a big way and that you have no worries at all. Those little things you want will seem smaller and smaller when you realize all you already have.

You'll start seeing things differently and thinking

straight. Those cracks in your foundation will be repaired, and when you choose peace over worry, you'll quickly realize you've made a better decision.

Tips to Overcome Worry

If you're still thinking that you just can't help worrying, then let's try to give you something else to do with your time. After all, you might not be able to help worrying, but God can help you if you really want to get past it.

Here are some ideas.

Take one day at a time.

Let's say you have a hundred dollars in your "life" bank account for today. Each time you worry, you use some of your money for the day. You use a little of it just getting up and getting dressed and prepared for the day. You use some thinking about the test you're having at school or the tryouts for the school play, and so now you have eighty dollars left for the day, and it's only eight a.m.

By ten a.m., you discover your friend Jenny is mad at you, and you totally forgot to turn in your science paper from when you were out sick last week. Your teacher is unhappy with you, and now you've got sixty dollars left in your life bank account.

Before noon, you're worrying about how you can get that science paper done when you know your family is going out for the evening. You've still got the history test later in the afternoon, and you're not sure you're prepared for it. You know your dad will be pretty angry if you get another  grade that he thinks is less than your best effort. Now the day's not even half over, and you've only got thirty dollars left in your life bank account.

While you're walking home from school, you're worrying so much, you don't see the kid coming at you on the sidewalk on his bike, and you have to jump out of his way. You fall and get your pants all stained. Nothing is going right today!

Down to Your Last Ten Bucks

Mom tells you to take the dog out for a walk when you get home, and the dog runs off without you. You have to spend time chasing him, and you still have homework to do. Now you're down to only ten dollars left in your life bank account.

You've literally used up most of your dollars worrying throughout the day. How can you make a deposit and get things back on track before you are at zero?

What to Do When You're Spent

Before you go to sleep at night, go back through your day. When could you have added to your bank account? When could you have chosen to do something other than worry?

You could have started your day with a prayer. You could have thanked God for being with you through the night and asked for His help with your day as you took the test and went through the tryouts for the play. You could have thanked Him again for helping you and walked out the door.

When you discovered your friend was mad at you, you could have chosen to find out the problem and tried to solve it quickly. You could have set up a time to talk with her and decide how things should be handled. You would have been actively trying to solve the problem rather than simply worrying about it.

Same with the science paper. You could have offered to stay in at lunchtime and finish the paper, or set up a time with your teacher to complete it first thing in the morning or after school. Whatever the solution, you would not have had to worry about it. And instead of emptying your life bank account, you could have been adding to it.

You get the point. You can totally run out of steam to handle things if you spend every moment in worry. Take care of the things you can and leave the rest to God. And taking time to pray can put things in perspective. It may give you fresh ideas to handle things or just get your mind refocused on God. Remembering how faithful and awesome God is can always fix worry.

You can speak the Word of God out loud.
If you memorize a few Bible verses in your life, this is one that will help you when you're tempted to worry. It's Philippians 4:6, 7 (NCV), and it says this:

Do not worry about anything, but pray and ask God for everything you need, always giving thanks. And

God's peace, which is so great we cannot understand it, will keep your hearts and minds in Christ Jesus.

So you see the answer. Talk to God, tell Him what you need, and thank Him for caring about you and being with you. You have His Word on it!

Give your cares to God and stand strong.

Worry makes you weaker and weaker. It robs you of your joy and your strength. Look at what 1 Peter 5: 6–9 tells you.

Be humble under God's powerful hand so he will lift you up when the right time comes. Give all your worries to him, because he cares about you. Control yourselves and be careful! The devil, your enemy, goes around like a roaring lion looking for someone to eat. Refuse to give in to him, by standing strong in your faith. You know that your Christian family all over the world is having the same kinds of suffering.

This is why it's so important for you to watch what you're thinking. When you're feeling weak, stand strong in the faith that God will help you win the battle.

Take a break and rest in God's hand.

Worry is like a loud and obnoxious sound that keeps going on. You need to put in earplugs so you can hear. Worry says all kinds of mean things to you and keeps you paying attention because of its noise. But when you block it out and listen for God, worry cannot distract you.

Pull the Plug on Worry

Stop the noise! Pull the plug on worry! Don't listen to it anymore. Instead, choose to listen to God's Word. That might mean reading the Bible or listening to worship music that reminds you of His peace and

love. And while you're listening to that, rest in God's care and grace.

Jesus told you in John 14:27:

I leave you peace; my peace I give you. I do not give it to you as the world does. So don't let your hearts be troubled or afraid.

Jesus did not worry, and you don't have to worry, either!

Make up your mind that worry is a waste of time.
Even after you read this book, you'll probably still worry about things. It seems to be human nature. It doesn't have to be your nature, though. You can choose to think that worry is a waste of time. All these Scriptures in the Bible are trying to tell you that. When you're tempted to worry, go back and read these verses again and again until they are more important to you than anything you might be worrying about. Make up your mind, and you'll feel better on the inside.

Look at Hebrews 13:5. God says:

"...I will never leave you; I will never forget you." So we can be sure when we say, "I will not be afraid,

because the Lord is my helper: People can't do anything to me."

Do you see how God watches over you? Do you realize that God sees all the details of your life?

If it's a concern to you, it's a concern to Him. There isn't one thing in your life that God does not care about—He loves and wants to help you with everything!

You do your part, and God will do His part. You can depend on Him—that's His promise to you!

Chapter 10

Making Judgments

Have you ever judged someone before you really got to know him or her? Chances are you have, because we all have. But, judging others is a mistake.

For example, you see a new kid at church. You can tell that she's new because she doesn't dress like all of the other kids at church. Her shirt is dirty and even has a few holes (and not *cute* ones, either). Her hair is very messy and looks like she hasn't washed it in weeks. No one comes to your church looking like that. You judge this girl right away and decide to stay away from her—after all, she might not smell good.

But later in the service, the youth pastor introduces the strange girl. Apparently she is visiting from another country. She says she dressed like this on purpose to get your attention. She says some of the kids in her country dress like this because they do not have a lot of running water to wash their clothes, their hair, or even themselves. She talks a lot about her country, and it sounds interesting. She says even more and more people are learning about Jesus and accepting Him as their Savior. She says faith is growing in her country, and people are happy. She thanks your youth pastor for inviting her and lets you know that your donations have really been helping her and her people.

Whoa, you feel awful now. You just prayed for the people in her country last week. You wish you had saved your judgment about the girl.

Judges

It's not always easy to spot them, but the judges are out there all the time. We don't realize how closely they might look at what we do and what we say and what we wear, but it happens all the time. And sometimes, *we* are the judges.

The Bible tells us in Matthew:

Don't judge other people, or you will be judged. You will be judged in the same way that you judge others, and the amount you give to others will be given to you. Why do you notice the little piece of dust in your friend's eye, but you don't notice the big piece of wood in your own eye? How can you say to your friend, "Let me take that little piece of dust out of your eye?" Look at yourself! You still have that big piece of wood in your own eye. You hypocrite!

First, take the wood out of your own eye. Then you will see clearly to take the dust out of your friend's eye. (Matthew 7:1–5)

Let's look at this Scripture and see how it can help us.

Why Do We Judge Others?

Some of the reasons may look like this:

■ We think someone else just doesn't know the rules…our rules, that is.

- We think that we have the answer, and we want to share it.
- We want others to know how smart we are.
- We want others to look up to us.
- We want to feel good about ourselves.
- We believe it's our job to set others straight about things. (That's called "arrogant pride.")
- We think we're providing a needed service.
- We don't stop to think that we could be wrong.
- It's easier to tell others what's wrong with them than it is to take an honest look at ourselves.
- We forget Rule Number One: Love one another!

No doubt we could keep this list going, but let's think about some of the points based on what Matthew has to say.

The Two-Edged Sword of Judgment

Right off the bat, we're told to "stop judging others." You're probably thinking that you've always been taught that you should judge others so you can decide if you should make friends with them or not. You think of that as just being wise. Well, we're not really talking about choosing friends here. We're talking about what we sometimes do to both friends and complete strangers alike.

Sending in the Judge

The Scripture in Matthew is about those moments when we're critical of others in ways that aren't fair. It might be an innocent judgment about someone's hair, their outfit, or their attitude. It's okay to have an opinion and keep it to yourself, but if you feel a need to comment on it to the person or to someone else, the trouble begins. It really gets bad when you treat the person differently or badly because of your "judgment." The Bible says, "Don't judge other people, or you will be judged."

Now, that's interesting! Do you think it means that as soon as you pass a judgment about how someone looks today, coming down the hallway is someone who is going to pass that same judgment on you?

The judging game is not a good game to play because when you judge and are critical of others, they are also being critical and judgmental about you. You just became the next person to be judged! The funny part is that no one has a right to do the judging, anyway. The only One who is qualified to judge is God!

Getting the Log Out

The thing to look at when judging others is how we "see" others.

We think someone else's little problem needs to be corrected by us, because we don't want anyone to notice we have a big problem ourselves. We're blind to our own faults.

We give ourselves excuses to behave badly. But in Romans 2, the Bible says that we have no excuse for our behavior when we judge others, because we do the same things ourselves. That log, or piece of wood, is jammed in our eyes, and we can't see ourselves. Take a moment and imagine a log jammed into your eye. Can you see anything?

Logjams

Have you ever noticed that when you're in a good mood, the world looks much brighter? You're nicer to the people around you, more forgiving, kinder?

What happens when you're in a bad mood about something? You're mad, frustrated, and hard to get along with. You think everyone should see things your way, and you only see the bad things in those around you. That's when you're dealing with a logjam. That's when you're not even able to feel or see the judge that lurks within you. Your eyes are filled with that big piece of wood.

Having Good Judgment

Please understand that in this whole chapter about judgment, we're not talking about having good judgment. We're not talking about the things you know that you should do to be safe and to be careful of yourself and others. We're talking about the things that are triggered in your mind that give you an excuse to think bad thoughts about other people.

Plain and simple, judging people is mean and will not help you be a good friend to others or help show people what a believer in God looks like.

How Do You Keep the Judge Away?

- You stop making excuses for your behavior when you make quick judgments about others.
- You take another look at yourself
- You look for the good in others.
- You ask God to show you what you need to understand about the way you're thinking.
- You check your heart and your "love meter" to see if your thinking is coming from the right place.
- You look at your trust level for others and see if you need to change some things.
- You look at your friendships and try to be kinder.
- You give God the thanks for being the One who handles all the stuff you don't understand about other people.
- You give up your need to let others know how "right" you are.
- You take the log out of your own eye first.

Seeing More Clearly

You've been blessed. You are a child of God. Look at what the Bible says in 2 Peter 1:5–9 NCV:

> *Because you have these blessings, do your best to add these things to your lives: to your faith, add goodness; and to your goodness, add knowledge; and to your knowledge, add self-control; and to your self-control, add patience; and to your patience, add service for God; and to your service for God, add kindness for your brothers and sisters in Christ; and to this kindness, add love. If all these things are in you and are growing, they will help you to be useful and productive in your knowledge of our Lord Jesus Christ. But anyone who does not have these things cannot see clearly. He is blind and has forgotten that he was made clean from his past sins.*

Taking the log out of your own eye will help you see more clearly. Taking a moment to think before you cast judgment on anyone else will help you be more loving and kind. You are growing in God every day. Let your heart guide your thoughts and keep you always in His love.

Be Kind to Yourself, Too

Remember, too, that as you think good thoughts about others, it's okay to think good thoughts about yourself as well. Talking nicely to yourself is a loving thing to do. Sometimes the judge in you is way too hard on yourself. If you find that is happening, go back and apply all the tools you would use to be kinder to others and use them for yourself. That will help you see things more clearly. And you may discover the log has disappeared.

Chapter 11

Change Your Mind!

Hey, Are We There Yet?

You've probably been on a few trips with your parents that seemed to go on and on. Maybe you got stuck in traffic or the scenery was just not that impressive, and even after taking a nap, you wake up to find that you still haven't reached your destination. Finally, you can't stand it, and you call out, "Are we there yet?"

The Children of Israel Ask, "Are We There Yet?"

Now, step back in history and try to imagine the children of Israel as they wandered around on their way to the Promised Land. Unlike you, they didn't have a chest packed with ice, sandwiches, and drinks. They didn't even have their choice of fast-food restaurants at every exit. Instead, they had the hot desert, worn-out sandals, and manna and quail to keep them alive and well. A little different scene, but some little kid riding a donkey for more than two years probably asked the same question: "Are we there yet?"

Trouble is, they weren't there! In fact, they drove their herds around for forty years, and most of them never did get there. The whole trip should have taken them eleven days, but it took them forty years (see Deuteronomy 1:2). You have to wonder what they were thinking!

Anyway, the point is that you will go through seasons of wandering as well. You may even have some wilderness thinking going on right now. What are you going to do about it? Imagine, if you're ten years old now as you read this book, and if it takes you forty years to understand God's direction, you'll be fifty before you even start to get on course. Whoa! Don't let that happen to you!

So let's do some wilderness training right now. That is the training it takes to keep you from wandering in the wilderness of your own life.

What Is Wilderness Thinking?

In some ways, wilderness thinking is "stuck" thinking. It's when you can't see another way to go, no matter where you look. God finally had to speak to the children of Israel. He said, "You have stayed at this mountain long enough. It is time to break camp and move on" (Deuteronomy 1:6–7 NLT).

Can you think of any time when God might say that to you? "Look, you've walked around your reason for being mad at your friend long enough, move on." Or, "You've kept your worries to yourself long enough, let's talk about them." You see, you can get stuck in "stinkin' thinkin'." You can be in a place that your mind has no business being and just sit there without making any progress. Stop! It's time to move on.

Let's get out of the wilderness as quickly as possible.

Getting Closer to the Promised Land

Pretend you're going to do an oil painting in your art class at school. The teacher has given you the freedom to paint anything you want as long as it means something to you and it's something you'll be proud to put in the school art show. Let's also assume that you love to paint, and this is a really exciting opportunity for you.

How do you start? Chances are, before you begin to draw or paint anything, you start with a vision, a plan. You think about all the subjects you might like to paint. Maybe you'll paint the backyard scenery behind your house or try to copy an old photograph. You start by thinking clearly about what you want to do. You cannot create anything, much less a masterpiece, without a plan.

Are You Ready to Paint?

Maybe, or maybe not! You have a great idea, but now doubt has come into your head. You're pretty sure you're not a very good artist and you won't be able to do it. You set your mind up for failure. You start to complain that you don't have the right paint colors and your brush is not very good. You tell yourself that you can't do this.

Are you starting to hear the children of Israel complaining in the background? Can you hear them whining that they should have just stayed in Egypt because now they aren't so sure they can make it?

What's Your Mind-set?

If you start with a mind-set that says you can't do it, guess what? You won't be able to do it. That's right! If you want to do anything ever, you have to believe that it is something you can do. God has given you many gifts, and He wants you to use them. He believes you can paint.

If you start grumbling and complaining and becoming miserable over your painting, your vision will fade. You will forget what you wanted to do, because you will be taking your eyes off the goal. You'll just be looking at what isn't perfect and putting more focus on what you can't do versus what you can do. And the target you focus on the longest is the thing you usually hit.

Step past your painting for a moment and look at life in general. How do you get out of wilderness thinking about anything in life?

Steps to Try:

- Create a plan.
- Believe in your ability to carry out the plan.
- Have an attitude of gratitude.
- Think about where you're going, not where you've been.
- Look for God's help and guidance.
- Remind yourself of your first idea, your plan.
- Get the job done!

Changing Your Mind Is Like Changing Your Socks... Sort Of!

If you've ever been in the same room with someone who didn't change their socks for a day or two, or maybe longer, you may have noticed a certain ugly smell in the air. You may have even asked, "What stinks?" Stinky socks are not unlike stinky thoughts. You need to change both of them as fast as possible.

The Stinky Sock Wars

Let's say your brother just came in from playing basketball in the hot sun, and he's all sweaty. He takes off his sneakers, and the most horrible smell whips across the room and hits you right in the nose. You suggest rather loudly that he should go change his socks or maybe take a shower. It seems very reasonable. But...he doesn't feel like it right then.

Somebody Do It for Me!

He looks at you and says, "Hey, if it bothers you so much, go get me some clean socks and take these stinky ones to the laundry room. I don't feel like doing it right now."

You know if you do it, things will be more pleasant for you, but there's no way you're touching those smelly socks. So you decline and keep complaining. You finally take the issue to a higher court: You complain to Mom.

Those Wilderness Children

The children of Israel did the same thing. When things didn't go their way, they complained to Moses. Moses said prayers for them. He kept asking God to help them, but God was getting a little upset with the lazy children for not appreciating anything He'd already done for them. He expected them to be responsible to do the job at hand.

He expects the same thing of you! When your mind is cluttered with things that need to be changed or washed or tossed out completely, you need to get ready for a new mind-set. You've got to be responsible for what you think. You've got to get things cleaned out so you can have a clean mind-set. You might stay in the wilderness if you don't.

God Will Lead You Forward

God will lead you, guide you, and tell you what direction to go, but you need to do the walking. He can't do it all for you. You have an important part to play yourself. Whether you're making some new decisions because you've been stuck on old ones, or whether you're creating a new plan for your life, you need to take the action steps yourself. Only you can paint that masterpiece. Without your brush, the canvas remains blank.

Putting It Off Till Later

In our previous little story of your brother with the stinky socks, we saw the reason that putting something off till later is not a very good answer. When you're tempted to do that, maybe you should picture those smelly socks sitting right next to you. You know that means you have to do something—even if it's just to get away from the smell.

The Time Is Now!

When you're trying to do something as difficult as changing your mind, you might be tempted to· put it aside until tomorrow. Then you might think that it can't hurt to wait a few more days. Lots of people do that about prayer. They mean to pray—they just never seem to find the time. The time is now!

Whatever it is that needs to be changed when you're out there in the desert, it needs to be changed right away. You're already thirsty. You know when you're hot and thirsty and the ice-cream truck starts playing its music as it comes down your street. What happens if you don't run right away and grab your dollar for a cone? That's right, the truck goes on without you.

You Missed the Ice-Cream Truck

The same thing can happen in other areas of life, too. You can wait too long, and the chance to change things will pass you by. You'll have to wait a long time, and an eleven-day journey can end up taking you forty years. Your ice-cream cone will melt.

If you keep your allowance in a jar in your room and you know it's okay for you to get ice cream when the truck comes by, then you're prepared and ready to get what you want. If you haven't planned ahead, you still might not be ready, even if you see the truck coming. God wants you to always be ready to receive the gifts He has for you.

In my book for adults, I give them ten different ways that they can be having a hard time with "stinkin' thinkin'." The list tries to show the ways we talk to ourselves and to others when we're not thinking very well. I've changed it a little bit for you.

The Stinkin' Thinkin' List (This is a list of things NOT to say)

1. It's too late to change my future!
2. I want someone else to take care of it!
3. Everything is just too hard!
4. I can't help it—I'm just a kid!
5. I want it now!
6. It's not my fault!
7. Poor me! Poor me!
8. God doesn't really love me!
9. Other kids have more than I do!
10. I'll do it my way!

Did I miss any of the excuses you use to stay stuck? If I did, you can add them to the list yourself.

We'll look at one more wilderness thought and then go on. One of the biggest roadblocks to ever winning at life is the one that says, "Everything is too hard, so I think I'll give up!" Did you ever use that one?

Breaking Those Bad Habits

You know what a bad habit is: It's something you do that is not good for you. You've often heard your parents remind you, "Don't forget to wash your hands!" And they don't tell you that because it's fun to remind you a hundred times to do it. They remind you because when you wash your hands, you remove all the bad germs that have the potential to make you sick. If you don't wash your hands and you keep getting sick, it's possible that this bad habit is playing a part.

So don't think about breaking bad habits as a bad thing—it is ultimately for your own good!

It Gets Harder to Remember!

The hardest part about breaking that bad habit is to remember to do it. That means taking the time to slow down, think about what you are thinking about, remember what your parents said, and then do it. And if you don't get it right away, that's okay! Just stick with it, and ask God to help you remember.

Sure, you've got a lot going on and you want to get back outside to play with your friends, but either you take the time to wash your hands now, or you might get sick from the germs on your hands, and then you

won't be able to play with your friends for a couple days while you are inside getting better.

Romans 5:3–5 says:

We also have joy with, our troubles, because we know that these troubles produce patience. And patience produces character, and character produces hope. And this hope will never disappoint us, because God has poured out his love to fill our hearts.

So, don't lose heart, don't give up...hang in there! You can clean up your act, change your mind, and get rid of those bad habits. You can do it, because God will help you!

Chapter 12

The Blame Game

Y ou probably don't do this, but some people like to make excuses for why they made a bad choice. They come up with reasons why they didn't listen to their parents or get their homework done or go to piano practice. They ignore the fact that God is even part of their lives.

Our goal in this chapter is to give you some tools to

help fix the problems that come up in your life without putting the blame on others. If you can learn to fix your thoughts on the truth of the Holy Spirit, then you won't be tempted to make excuses. Let's take a look at some all too human examples from the Bible.

Finding Someone Else to Blame

God knows us so well. This goes all the way back to Adam and Eve in the Garden. The first people to get caught doing something they were specifically told not to do handled it by fixing the blame. Let's look at Adam's response when God was trying to find them in the Garden.

> But the LORD God called to the man and said, "Where are you?" The man answered, "I heard you walking in the garden, and I was afraid because I was naked, so I hid."
>
> God asked, "Who told you that you were naked? Did you eat fruit from the tree from which I commanded you not to eat?"
>
> The man said, "You gave this woman to me and she gave me fruit from the tree, so I ate it." Then the Lord God said to the woman, "How could you have done such a thing?"

She answered, "The snake tricked me, so I ate the fruit." (Genesis 3:9–13)

Hey, It Wasn't My Fault!

Do you see what happened? No one took personal responsibility for their actions. They instantly blamed each other. Adam blamed God because God had given him the woman. Then he blamed the woman because she gave him the fruit. Eve blamed the snake because she felt tricked by the whole thing. What was the result? They felt naked before God. In other words, they felt like God could see right through them.

Have you ever been caught in a moment where you weren't telling the whole truth? If so, you might know what that feels like. They were ashamed of themselves, but they couldn't even admit it.

GOD aLways Loves You!

One more point to make in this story is this: God was angry with Adam and Eve for what they did.

However, just a bit further down in Genesis, we read that even though God punished them, He also immediately started to help them. He made clothes for them and provided for their needs.

The point is that, even when you sin, God forgives and works with you to help you not sin again. That can only happen when you admit the truth, fix your eyes and heart on Him, and work with Him to work things out.

The Excuses!

Whenever you find yourself ashamed of something you've done, or something you've maybe even left undone, your mind races to find a way out. Like Adam and Eve, you run for the bushes, hoping not to be discovered. That's when the excuses show up. It always makes you feel better about doing wrong if you have a reason you can give for wrong behavior. It's how we trick ourselves—and how Satan tricks us, too.

What Kinds of Excuses Do We Give?

- I did it because my friend did it!
- No one told me I couldn't do it!
- I don't feel good!
- I couldn't help it!
- I didn't think it was such a big deal!
- All my friends do it!
- I saw Dad do it!
- Everybody wants me to be like my sister!
- The dog chewed my homework paper!
- The alarm didn't go off on time!
- Everybody else gets to do it!
- I had too much sugar!
- Mom didn't remind me!
- I'm just a kid!

You can add to this list of excuses, or you can start taking responsibility for your actions. Just because the blame game is played all the time doesn't mean you have to participate. You can even stop playing.

How Do You Stop the Blame Game?

- You can come out of the bushes. You don't need to hide from yourself or from God.
- You can face the truth. You can look at yourself in the mirror and admit what you did wrong. You can be the one to own the wrong.
- You can check to see how you really feel about what you did wrong. If you're sad about it and wish you had not done it, you can...
- Turn to God and ask His forgiveness. You don't have to give Him your old excuses because He's not interested in "why" you did it. He's interested in what you want to do now to make amends. He's interested in what your heart has learned.
- You can accept God's forgiveness and ask for His help in not allowing you to do that kind of wrong again. That's part of what we ask every day in the Lord's Prayer (which we'll talk about shortly).
- If you've hurt someone in your wrongdoing, you can now go to that person and ask him or her to forgive you. Sometimes you might even need to try to make amends, like replacing a broken or stolen item.

If you're not that familiar with the Lord's Prayer, it goes like this: Jesus said to his followers, "Your Father knows the things you need before you ask him." So when you pray, you should pray like this:

> *Our Father in heaven,*
> *may your name always be kept holy.*
> *May your kingdom come*
> *and what you want be done,*
> *here on earth as it is in heaven.*
> *Give us the food we need for each day.*
> *Forgive us for our sins,*
> *just as we have forgiven those who sinned against us.*
> *And do not cause us to be tempted,*
> *but save us from the Evil One.*
>   *Matthew 6:8–13 (from the NCV)*

When your mind is not sure what to do, stop first and pray this prayer. God will help you before you make a mistake.

Also, in John 8:32, Jesus said, "If you continue to obey my teaching, you are truly my followers. Then you will know the truth, and the truth will make you free."

How Can Truth Set You Free?

What does it mean to be free of something? Anything? Let's think of examples:

- If you don't have homework after school, you're free to go play.
- If you finish your chores at home, you're free to watch TV.
- If you ask someone to forgive you and they do, your heart feels better.
- If you admit something to yourself that wasn't really true, you're free to discover what the truth really is.
- If you have time to yourself, you're free to choose how to spend it.

After being set free, you will be able to look back and see how certain things were working in your mind to keep you captured. You're free to explore, to rejoice, to sing, to celebrate, to play, to work, to give, to receive. That is the variety of gifts that comes with being set free.

Your own mind can be the prison, and it can make you a slave. You can think in such a way that you have

no freedom at all. That's usually the time when you've allowed the excuses to come in and live there.

But the truth sets you free! And when you're free, you're free indeed! Every time you embrace the truth, let it guide you, and let it lead you, you're free. God is truth, and He will always set you free!

Doing It Your Way!

One final thing I'd really like you to think about is this: You live in a world today that applauds you if you do things your own way: You get credit for being first or best or smartest. All of those things are fine, but sometimes they cause you to forget another truth. That truth is that you belong to God and not to yourself.

Psalm 78:4–8 NLT says:

We will not hide these truths from our children but will tell the next generation about the glorious deeds of the Lord. We will tell of his power and the mighty miracles he did. For he issued a decree to Jacob; he gave his law to Israel. He commanded our ancestors to teach them to their children, so the next generation might know them-even the children not yet born-that they in turn might teach their children.

So each generation can place their hope in God, remembering his glorious miracles and obeying his commands. Then they will not be like their ancestors-stubborn, rebellious, and unfaithful, refusing to give their hearts to God.

God wants you to have a very positive attitude. He wants you to know all the good things He has planned for your life. He wants you to give your heart and mind and soul to Him so that He can fill your life with good things. He wants your thoughts to be directed toward Him in everything you do.

A Prayer for You

Please pray this prayer with me that God will protect your heart and mind and help you be a winner on the battlefield for your thoughts. Now is such a great time to learn how to be strong so you can win the battle your whole life through. And know that I will be praying for you—you've got this!

Dear Lord, please watch over [put your name here]. Please strengthen his/her heart and mind toward You. Please help him/her win the battle. Bless all that he/she does to learn more about You and to grow in spirit according to Your will and Your mercy. I thank you God, today for this wonderful kid. Bless him/her with loving and obedient thoughts every day. Amen.

Isaiah 55:6–9 NLT reminds us about how the Lord thinks and what He wants from you. Let's take a look:

Seek the LORD while you can find him. Call on him now while he is near. Let the people turn from their wicked deeds. Let them banish from their minds the very thought of doing wrong! Let them turn to the

LORD that he may have mercy on them. Yes, turn to our God, for he will abundantly pardon.

"My thoughts are completely different from yours," says the LORD. *"And my ways are far beyond anything you could imagine. For just as the heavens are higher than the earth, so are my ways higher than your ways and my thoughts higher than your thoughts."*

Have Good Thoughts!

May all your thoughts build you up and make you smile before the Lord. Be His kid in every way you think and every way you act. If you do, He will bless you forever.

Thanks for sharing this book with me. My prayers, my thoughts, and my heart are with you.

If you have not accepted Jesus—or you don't know if you have—pray this prayer with me. Then talk with your parents or another Christian you trust.

Jesus, I know that I have sinned and am in need of a Savior.

I believe that when you went to the Cross, you went there for me and all my sins.

I trust You to save me right now. I give you my life.

Today, I know I'm saved and that You forgive me, but help me to understand what it means to live for you every day. Amen.

If you have never accepted Jesus, I would love to pray with you now. God says in His Word in Romans 10:9 that if we confess to the Lord our God and believe in our hearts that God raised His son Jesus from the dead, we shall be saved. Today, if you feel like Jesus is calling you to a personal relationship with Him, and you are ready to follow His leadership in everything that you do, pray this out loud:

Jesus, I know that I have sinned and am in need of a Savior.

I believe that when you went to the Cross, you went there for me and all my sins.

I trust You to save me right now. I give you my life.

Today, I know I'm saved and that You forgive me, but help me to understand what it means to live for you every day. Amen.

About the Author

JOYCE MEYER is one of the world's leading practical Bible teachers. A *New York Times* bestselling author, Joyce's books have helped millions of people find hope and restoration through Jesus Christ. Joyce's programs, *Enjoying Everyday Life* and *Everyday Answers with Joyce Meyer,* air around the world on television, radio, and the Internet. Through Joyce Meyer Ministries, Joyce teaches internationally on a number of topics, with a particular focus on how the Word of God applies to our everyday lives. Her candid communication style allows her to share openly and practically about her experiences so others can apply what she has learned to their lives.

Joyce has authored more than a hundred books, which have been translated into more than one hundred languages, and over 65 million of her books have been distributed worldwide. Bestsellers include *Power Thoughts*; *The Confident Woman*; *Look Great, Feel Great*; *Starting Your Day Right*; *Ending Your Day Right*; *Approval Addiction*; *How to Hear from God*; *Beauty for Ashes*; and *Battlefield of the Mind*.

Joyce's passion to help hurting people is foundational

to the vision of Hand of Hope, the missions arm of Joyce Meyer Ministries. Hand of Hope provides worldwide humanitarian outreach such as feeding programs, medical care, orphanages, disaster response, human trafficking intervention and rehabilitation, and much more—always sharing the love and Gospel of Christ.

JOYCE MEYER MINISTRIES U.S. & FOREIGN OFFICE ADDRESSES

Joyce Meyer Ministries
P.O. Box 655
Fenton, MO 63026
USA
(636) 349-0303

Joyce Meyer Ministries—Canada
P.O. Box 7700
Vancouver, BC V6B 4E2
Canada
(800) 868-1002

Joyce Meyer Ministries—Australia
Locked Bag 77
Mansfield Delivery Centre
Queensland 4122
Australia
(07) 3349 1200

Joyce Meyer Ministries—England
P.O. Box 1549
Windsor SL4 1GT
United Kingdom
01753 831102

Joyce Meyer Ministries—South Africa
P.O. Box 5
Cape Town 8000
South Africa
(27) 21-701-1056

OTHER BOOKS BY JOYCE MEYER

La Dosis de Aprobación (The Approval Fix)

Empezando Tu Día Bien (Starting Your Day Right)

Hazte Un Favor a Ti Mismo...Perdona (Do Yourself a Favor...Forgive)

Madre Segura de sí Misma (The Confident Mom)

Pensamientos de Poder (Power Thoughts)

Termina Bien tu Día (Ending Your Day Right)

Usted Puede Comenzar de Nuevo (You Can Begin Again)

¡Viva con esperanza! (Get Your Hopes Up!)

Viva Valientemente (Living Courageously)

* Study Guide available for this title

BY DAVE MEYER

Life Lines

The BATTLEFIELD of the MIND
family of books
by #1 *New York Times* bestselling
author Joyce Meyer

Battlefield of the Mind

Readers will learn how to overcome negative thoughts with this multimillion-copy bestseller. They will gain control over their minds, become more patient, and conquer the damaging thoughts that try to steal their joy each day.

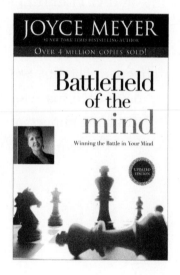

Battlefield of the Mind
Study Guide

(Revised Edition)

This thought-provoking, companion study guide will help readers maximize the power of what you learn in BATTLEFIELD OF THE MIND, with stirring questions, effective prompts, and designated space for journaling important reflections.

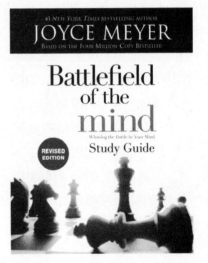

Battlefield of the Mind
for Teens

Joyce Meyer partners with popular author and speaker Todd Hafer to bring her respected wisdom and sound advice to today's teens—a group that desperately needs to hear Joyce's message. Using contemporary language, well-timed humor, powerful statistics, and teen-appropriate applications and calls to action, this book offers teens a relevant and engaging version of the bestselling original.

Battlefield of the Mind
Bible

With notes and commentary based on Joyce's all-time bestseller, *Battlefield of the Mind*, this Amplified Bible and Joyce's reflections helps readers overcome the thought battles they face each day and achieve a life-changing sense of peace and joy. Available in hardcover, paperback, and beautiful Euroluxe bindings in blue, pink, and brown.

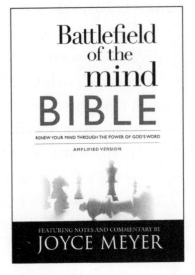

Battlefield of the Mind
Devotional

Daily inspiration and encouragement readers need to defeat the enemy and be victorious in the battle to transform their thinking.

Available wherever books are sold.